Dear Re...

The b... ...ler from St. ... *The New Yo...* ...ch month, we offer you a fascinating account of the latest, most sensational crime that has captured the national attention. St. Martin's is the publisher of perennial best-selling true crime author Jack Olsen whose SALT OF THE EARTH is the true story of one woman's triumph over life-shattering violence; Joseph Wambaugh called it "powerful and absorbing." Fanny Weinstein and Melinda Wilson tell the story of a beautiful honors student who was lured into the dark world of sex for hire in THE COED CALL GIRL MURDER. St. Martin's is also proud to publish critically acclaimed author Carlton Stowers, whose 1999 Edgar Award-winning TO THE LAST BREATH recounts a two-year-old girl's mysterious death and the dogged investigation that led loved ones to the most unlikely murderer: her own father. In the book you now hold, THE MOTHER'S DAY MURDER, veteran true crime writer Wensley Clarkson details the story of a husband and wife whose disastrous marriage would have murderous consequences.

St. Martin's True Crime Library gives you the stories *behind* the headlines. Our authors take you right to the scene of the crime and into the minds of the most notorious murderers to show you what really makes them tick. St. Martin's True Crime Library paperbacks are better than the most terrifying thriller, because it's all true! The next time you want a crackling good read, make sure it's got the St. Martin's True Crime Library logo on the spine—you'll be up all night!

Charles E. Spicer, Jr.
Senior Editor, St. Martin's True Crime Library

The Key Players in
THE MOTHER'S DAY MURDER . . .

Gina Spann—the seductive wife and mother who wanted her husband dead

Kevin Spann—the unwitting husband shot in cold blood on Mother's Day of 1997

Larry Kelley—Gina's adoring teenage lover, who would do anything for his woman

Matthew Piazzi and **Gerald Horne**—Kevin Spann's teenage executioners, two friends Larry Kelley recruited to shoot the estranged husband

St. Martin's Paperbacks True Crime Library titles by Wensley Clarkson

Doctors of Death
Whatever Mother Says
Deadly Seduction
Slave Girls
Death at Every Stop
In the Name of Satan
Caged Heat
The Railroad Killer
The Mother's Day Murder

THE MOTHER'S DAY
MURDER

WENSLEY CLARKSON

St. Martin's Paperbacks

THE MOTHER'S DAY MURDER

Copyright © 2000 by Wensley Clarkson.

Cover photographs of people courtesy Augusta Police Department. Photograph of rose by Don Banks.

ISBN: 0-312-97411-6

Printed in the United States of America

St. Martin's Paperbacks edition / May 2000

St. Martin's Paperbacks are published by St. Martin's Press, 175 Fifth Avenue, New York, NY 10010.

10 9 8 7 6 5 4 3 2 1

AUTHOR'S NOTE

The central figure in this story, Gina Spann, changed her name three times due to her propensity for marriage. In an effort to avoid confusion, throughout the book she is referred to by whichever name she was using at the time.

Some of the dialogue represented in this book was constructed from available documents, some was drawn from courtroom testimony, and some was reconstituted from the memory of participants.

The names of four individuals in this book have been changed. Those pseudonyms are Jane Walsh, Jim Huggins, Michael Dunleavy, and Nathan Blake.

To Clare, for putting up with me all these years

NOTES OF GRATITUDE

The idea of using a leaden, dispassionate word like "acknowledgments" for this section cannot begin to express the depth of my feelings for the many individuals who have made this book possible. I owe them my deepest and most heartfelt gratitude.

First, to my literary manager Peter Miller and my editor Charles Spicer: Without them this book would never have happened. Their support and guidance have been very much appreciated. Then there is Frank Abatemarco, whose ideas always strike a perfect chord in helping me to focus my true crime epics in the right direction.

Then there are the townsfolk of Augusta, Georgia, who welcomed me with such enthusiasm and hospitality. They include: official court reporter Cindy Mason, attorney Michael C. Garrett, Senior Assistant District Attorney Nancy B. Johnson, attorney Maureen Floyd, DA Danny Craig, police investigator Jimmy Vowell, Shanna and Amanda Quick, Jason Swallow, Jody Pierce, Debbie Mcleskey, Denis Wright, *The Augusta Chronicle* and Fred Wehner.

Lastly, to Mark Sandelson and John Glatt for providing all the usual facilities that have made this and so many of my other books possible.

"Nobody loves me but my mother, and she could be jivin', too."

—B.B. King

THE MOTHER'S DAY
MURDER

MOTHER'S DAY, SUNDAY, MAY 11, 1997, 10:55 PM— AUGUSTA, GEORGIA

911: 911.

Caller: I need, uh, I, I, please, I really need an ambulance at 3805 . . .

911: What's your problem?

Caller: He's got blood everywhere. I don't know. I just walked in and there's blood everywhere.

911: Okay, what's that address?

Caller: 3805 Old Waynesboro Road.

911: You can't tell what happened?

Caller: I just walked in the door and there's blood everywhere and I took my son and I threw him in the car and I came to a pay phone . . . I went in the door and there's blood everywhere. My husband's on the floor.

911: Okay, is he breathing?

Caller: I don't know. I don't think so . . .

INTRODUCTION

The smooth functioning of the world depends on a mother's nurturing, raising and protection of her child. But mothers are not without their ferocious side.

Moms are supposed to make us suffer. It's their Darwinian function. They give birth to us. They set the standards and expect us to meet them. They teach us the skills we need to survive in the world before they force us out of their nest.

Carl Jung believed that attitudes towards all mothers were influenced by the innate human predisposition to think that certain qualities are exclusively a mother's.

According to Jung, the human unconscious holds up mothers as archetypes with both positive and negative qualities.

Mothers possess a wide range of attributes such as solitude, wisdom, fertility, feminism, sympathy, helpfulness and mystical powers countered by darkness, secretiveness, a desire to devour—and seductiveness.

While many of us see our real mother as solicitous and kind, we may also reluctantly concede that she is or was seductive. If we think she is magical and feminine, we may also believe she is secretive.

Just think of such diverse mothers as the Greek goddess Demeter, the Blessed Virgin Mary, the Hindu goddess Kali and the wicked stepmother of so many fairy tales. It is no surprise that we celebrate their existence.

The original Mother's Day, like all holidays, was of pagan origin and held in Asia Minor in honor of the goddess Cybele. She was known as the Great Mother, or the Mother of the Gods.

Cybele was involved in many bizarre rituals, which eventually led to her banishment by Rome.

So it was that the cult of the Great Mother was cruelly weakened even before the coming of Christ.

The poet and classicist Robert Graves saw the battle between the pagan Goddess and the Hebrew and Christian God to be fundamental to the development of Western civilization.

In his book *King Jesus*, Graves claimed this was proved because Jesus of Nazareth declared war on "The Female" or the White Goddess of Birth, Love and Death.

As the earliest known European deity, the White Goddess also appeared as the New, Full and Old Moon and was also called the Triple Goddess.

Christianity's male Trinity, said Graves, triumphed over the trinity of the Goddess. The Western male conquered the Eastern and agricultural female.

In victory, the institutional and patriarchal Holy Roman Catholic Church subsumed and welcomed its former opponents by calling itself "Mother Church."

That was when a form of Mother's Day returned in honor of the church. Then in the fifth century, devotion to the Virgin Mary emerged as a new Mother cult, with this Mother of God firmly replacing Cybele, the Mother of the Gods. Meanwhile, in the Celtic continent and British Isles, the powerful Goddess Brigit was replaced by St. Brigid, her Christian successor. Her sacred Mother's Day, which was connected with the ewes coming in to milk, became St. Brigid's Day.

Formal mother worship was never completely wiped out, so Mother's Day in the British Isles was merged into Mothering Day by the seventeenth century.

On the fourth Sunday of Lent, children returned home with small gifts and "mothering cakes"—fruitcake.

In America, the second Sunday in May was declared Mother's Day by congressional resolution in 1914. President Woodrow Wilson proclaimed mothers "the greatest source of the country's strength and inspiration."

But celebrating Mother's Day is not just about a mother's triumphs. For there is a certain brand of ferocity behind the goodness and caring nature of mothers.

PROLOGUE

The .38 caliber nickel-plated Taurus with a 3-inch barrel and black Pachmeye grips was loaded with three blue-tip ball-type bullets. The teenager nervously handed his 16-year-old friend the weapon as the two youths approached the single-story house. The younger boy gripped the gun tightly in his hand and panned it around for a few moments, just like he'd seen them do in the movies and on TV.

It was a quiet, warm Sunday night on Old Waynesboro Road, in Richmond County on the southeast edge of the sleepy city of Augusta, Georgia. Suddenly the headlights of a truck swept around the corner from a side street. The two youths ducked into the bushes by the side of the house so they wouldn't be caught in the full beams.

They waited for the throbbing V-8 to fade in the distance before moving back towards the front door. The younger, much smaller boy cocked the gun unsteadily. His 18-year-old friend knocked on the door and they waited. And waited. And waited.

The older youth tried again. This time much harder. The two teenagers heard movements inside the house, followed by the shuffling of feet towards the front door.

The boy's grip on the gun tightened. He was so tense he started to fear that he might pull the trigger too soon.

Then the latch inside the front door snapped and it opened gently. A bleary-eyed man in his mid-thirties in a T-shirt and jeans stood in front of the boys.

The schoolboy's finger squeezed tight on the trigger. The .38 exploded with a loud pop. The bullet entered the man's left cheek and exited out the back of his skull. Then the 16-year-old fired a second shot for good measure. That bullet entered through the neck, passed through the trachea and exited from the victim's back. His life had been snuffed out before his body had even crumpled to the floor.

The two youths looked at each other, eyes filled with terror, fear, excitement and a twisted sense of achievement. Then they snapped out of the trance, turned and ran and ran and ran.

A few minutes later Mrs. Gina Spann arrived at her home at 3805 Old Waynesboro Road, walked through the back door of the single-storey house and headed towards the front room where her husband often watched TV.

The first thing she noticed was that the front door was wide open. She moved across the room with slight trepidation, unsure if she really wanted to find out why.

Then she saw the corpse of her husband, Kevin,

crumpled on the floor of the entranceway. Blood was
pouring from the head wound. He wasn't moving and
she sensed the moment she looked at him that he must
be dead.

Every now and again headlights eerily lit up the
front room as cars sped past, blissfully unaware of the
tragedy that had just unfolded a few yards away.

Gina Spann leaned down to touch her husband.
There was no response but surely there was some-
thing she could do. She called out to him, "Kevin?
Kevin?"

Nothing.

Not far away those two youths were, in the words of
one, "pretty much haul[ing] ass" as they moved
swiftly across the roads and fields towards a local
wood to try and put as much distance as they could
between themselves and the cold-blooded crime they
had just committed.

As the two teenagers crept across one pitch-black
back yard a dog growled. It sounded very close by.
Suddenly they found themselves face to face with a
Rottweiler, baring yellow teeth that glistened in the
moonlight. The animal was coming in their direction.
The teenagers stood rooted to the spot in fear.

The Rottweiler leapt at them both but froze in mid-
air. It was only then they realized the animal was on
a chain and he was straining to get any closer than
one foot from them. The two youths swallowed nervously and headed off into the nearby fields.

A few minutes later, as they crossed through a
small wood, the 16-year-old silently pulled the .38 out
of his jacket and threw it towards a bunch of bushes.

The older youth never had a chance to say that they should have made more effort to hide the weapon.

Eventually they reached the other side of the wood and burst onto Tobacco Road panting and sweating. Faced with a public road and more familiar surroundings, the youths stopped running and began walking at a normal pace up the deserted highway.

A few hundred yards later they reached a pay phone and called a cab.

"We wanna go to Ryan's Steakhouse," the 16-year-old told the cab company operator.

"Kinda late for dinner, ain't it?" replied the operator.

Just a short distance away a distraught-sounding Mrs. Gina Spann was dialing 911 . . .

ONE

Gina Spann was born Gina Lynn Pierce in Belleville, Illinois, on January 12, 1966. Her mother Sue and father Steve led a reasonably quiet, uneventful life for the first few years of Gina's childhood—but then, not a lot happened in Belleville.

It was the sort of place where most folks minded their own business, got on with their jobs and raised a family. But in the middle of all this mediocrity stood Gina's father, Steve Pierce. His work barely brought in enough cash to pay for the family's three-bedroom home on a run-down street on the edge of town.

And when a baby boy, Steve Jr., arrived, followed shortly after by another daughter, Betty Jo, Steve Sr. began staying out nights, much to the irritation of his wife. It was his way of saying he couldn't cope.

It didn't take long for Sue Pierce to get wind of some of the gossip that began sweeping around town about her husband. She heard that not only was he picking fights in many of Belleville's seedier taverns but he was also making a habit of picking up stray women.

At first Sue Pierce chose to ignore the rumors and

hope that her husband would grow out of his behavior. But following the birth of Betty Jo, Steve Pierce's visits to Belleville's bars and flophouses increased two-fold. He was out all night at least twice a week and offering his wife no excuses when he stumbled in reeking of booze as the kids were waking up for school.

In the fall of 1973, Sue Pierce finally snapped and pointed an accusing finger at her cheating husband. Steve Pierce walked out of the house within days of that first confrontation and was never seen again. It was a devastating blow to his oldest child Gina. She'd reached an age when she knew how to charm her daddy, and he in turn believed she was the only spark of freshness in a troubled life that revolved around going to work, getting drunk and picking up women.

Young Gina had sensed things were not well for some time before the final split and, in the way that only needy children do, she'd tried to compensate for all the problems in the family home by talking to and amusing her father at every opportunity. That made his decision to abandon the family home a very difficult one for young Gina to accept.

Virtually every weekend for years following her father's departure she'd spend many hours wandering around Belleville in the hope of bumping into him. But she never saw him again.

As her sister Betty Jo later recalled: "I was so young I can hardly remember him. But Gina was heartbroken when her daddy ran out. She used to cry and cry at night. She so longed for him to come back but he never did."

Gina and her mom, brother and sister struggled on

but her father's desertion had a profound long-term effect. At the relatively young age of twelve Gina began regularly smoking cigarettes. While most youngsters did it to look cool, Gina needed the nicotine hits to calm her nerves. Her confidence was shattered by what had happened and those who were at school with her in the years after her father left home recall a quiet, painfully shy little girl who barely had the confidence to talk to anyone. "It was as if she was afraid to make friends with other kids in case they abandoned her," recalled one old school friend, Jane Walsh. But while Gina might not have fitted in socially, she became an honor roll student, first in grade school and then at Belleville East Junior High much to the delight of her family.

Then suddenly at the age of 16 she dropped out. No one in her family can even recall why it happened. Sue Pierce was so busy looking after the other two children and holding down a full-time job that she didn't have time to worry about such things.

"She just walked out one day. We couldn't get her to tell us why," recalled Betty Jo—known as Jody—Pierce. "Guess she just kinda gave up."

But to this day there is absolutely no suggestion of drugs or alcohol playing any part in Gina's problems. "She never drunk nothin' and drugs just weren't part of Gina's scene," recalled Jody. "She just flunked it."

As Gina's friend Jane Walsh explained: "You always knew there was a hell of a lot goin' on inside Gina's head but not all of it was directed towards her school work."

When Jane tried to talk to her about dropping out of school, Gina replied: "School's boring. I'm gonna find myself a man who'll look after me for the rest of my life."

Gina had watched her parents' marriage crumble but she genuinely believed that her life would improve if she could find the right partner, settle down and have kids.

During Gina's childhood, Mother's Day played a very special role in the Pierce household because Sue had worked so hard to keep her children's spirits up following her husband's walkout on the family.

Gina and her brother and sister would always put on a big show by making their mom a tasty breakfast and buying her gifts. Mother's Day became almost as important as birthdays to the Pierce children.

They knew their mom was often racked with guilt because she wasn't always there to ask how their day was when they returned from school, or to go over their homework or eat dinner with them.

"There was a lot of juggling going on inside that household. Sue had a job at a local diner that meant she sometimes worked long hours and the kids had to fend for themselves," said Jane Walsh.

Gina often found herself cooking and cleaning the house. It was something she grew to resent when she got older. Sometimes it felt that she was spending more time keeping the house in order than playing with her few friends. She was growing up too fast for her own good.

It would be wrong to claim that Gina's relationship with her mother was perfect throughout her childhood but every Mother's Day the past was forgotten and Gina thoroughly enjoyed organizing the Mother's

Day celebrations with her younger brother and sister.

Yet Mother's Day was also tinged with sadness for them. "It was the one day when we all realized just how much we wanted a father to be there for our mom," recalled sister Jody.

Gina's attitude was that if their father hadn't walked out on them they could have been enjoying a nice family day out instead of trying their hardest to compensate for the fact that he was permanently absent.

On Mother's Day every range of emotion kicked in for the Pierce kids. And they would never forget that.

Having flunked school, Gina was faced with the stark realization that she would have to get a job. She was not at all keen on the idea.

Gina preferred hanging out at home reading magazines and watching TV while her mom worked at the diner down the street and her brother and sister attended school.

Sue Pierce reluctantly agreed to this on condition that Gina keep the house tidy so her mom could relax after a hard day at work. But the more time Gina spent at home the less work she did to keep it clean.

"She got real lazy real fast," explained Jody. "She just couldn't be bothered."

And Gina got even more neglectful of the house when she began dating a soft-spoken local boy named Steve Hill. He had a job in a hardware store and would take Gina to drive-in movies and for the occasional burger. But since neither of them had much cash they stayed home watching TV most evenings.

Some of Gina's family members couldn't resist pointing out that Steve shared the same Christian name as her long-lost father. But, Gina told one friend, that was where the similarity ended.

Then in 1984 Gina got pregnant by Steve.

Gina believed that having a child was the key to her future happiness. She urged Steve to marry her, believing that he would have to support her and their child.

So, five months pregnant and just 18 years of age, Gina Pierce got married in a small civil ceremony in Belleville. A handful of friends and relatives attended. Many of them were relieved that Gina had found some real stability in her life.

Those who knew her at the time say that Gina was extremely happy about her new role in life as a homemaker and mother-to-be.

"She also saw it as a perfect way to avoid getting a job. Going straight from home to a domestic set-up with Steve Hill suited her perfectly," recalled Jody. "I guess it was a reaction to what had happened with Dad. She so longed to be part of a family unit that she decided to create her own."

Steve continued working in a local store and the couple lived together in a small rented apartment near her mom's home on the edge of Belleville. Gina told one friend that she would have liked to move to another town because it would have made a change. But they needed all the help they could get from Gina's mom and Steve's family. The couple rarely traveled outside the area because they couldn't afford vacations. Gina also told friends she didn't mind just so long as she and Steve had a family and "lived happily ever after." It was a recurring phrase in her life. The end of every fairy tale.

"Gina had this vision of how her life should turn out and she was determined to make it happen that way," says Jane Walsh.

At first married life seemed to make Gina more kind and considerate. Being pregnant put her in a good frame of mind. She liked the way people were more polite and respectful towards pregnant women. And she loved the sense of achievement.

But Gina could still be loud and extremely honest about her feelings. If she was upset at Steve she'd tell him. Steve Hill was a quiet, reserved character and took whatever she said with a grain of salt. Nothing seemed to faze him.

When Gina's baby eventually arrived on October 22, 1984, it seemed that stage one of her master plan for a happy, secure life was taking shape.

Her baby boy was named Michael. Gina even openly boasted that she intended to get pregnant again soon and hopefully she'd then have a daughter and her dream family would be complete. She'd enjoyed being pregnant. It made her glow inwardly and outwardly. It made her into an important person and she liked that.

The reality was not quite so perfect. Coming to terms with motherhood before she had had the opportunity to develop her own adult identity posed some acute problems.

Gina still had little self-confidence and virtually no real knowledge about childcare. She'd even admitted to one friend that she'd gotten pregnant partly because she wanted "to be loved by somebody." Steve's role in her life was already secondary in many ways.

However, Gina's wish to speedily get pregnant again came true. Just eleven months after the birth of Michael she had a baby girl who was christened Heather.

"Gina could hardly contain her pride," explained one relative. "She really felt as if she'd been blessed with good fortune."

Gina told her closest friends she wasn't worried that she'd waved good-bye to a career. It was more important to her to bring up a family, especially after what happened with her father.

But the speedy arrival of a second child did bring a certain level of stress to Gina and Steve's life because the families of both were worried that the couple would not be able to afford to bring up two children.

Gina acknowledged this was a problem and it created a level of tension between her and Steve because he was, not surprisingly, worried that Gina might get pregnant again—and that really would push them into a financial abyss.

In an effort to ease Steve's worries she agreed to go back into the hospital just eight weeks after Heather's birth to be sterilized. The operation was carried out at a medical center in nearby Fairview, Illinois.

"It seemed a natural step for Gina to take. She felt she'd got what she wanted and she knew they could never afford more than two kids. She was real practical in that way," says her sister Jody.

Many of Gina's school friends were at college by then but none of them were surprised by her marriage and children at such a young age. They saw Gina as a goodhearted earth momma type, raising kids, baking cakes and giving her husband a nice hot meal when he got home after a hard day's work. The reality was that Gina was more than just a tad sloppy around the house, and her idea of an afternoon's activity at home involved watching back-to-back soap operas rather than baking a few cookies.

Husband Steve seemed perfectly happy with this arrangement. But then, he was hardly in a position to complain. Gina made sure he got more than his fair share of attention.

That included providing him with regular sex— something that Gina had concluded was a daily requirement of her life.

Even in her teens Gina had had a healthy sexual appetite. A lot of it was due to the boredom of staying at home while others were out at school and work. All sorts of fantasies and sexual thoughts flowed through Gina's mind most days.

But she soon found that Steve wasn't very interested in their bedtime activities. He'd come up with all the old excuses of being too tired after a hard day at work, and Gina—who'd been stuck at home all day—found it extremely frustrating.

Gina, however, did not consider looking for sexual satisfaction elsewhere. As friend Jane Walsh explained: "Gina was actually pretty moral about cheating and stuff like that. She was determined not to end up doing the same as her father."

Life was very black-and-white for young mom-of-two Gina Hill. Her restricted education and tendency to stay in Belleville made sure of that.

Gina never once voiced any regret about missing out on college and all the sex, drugs, drink and rock'n'roll she could have experienced before settling down. In fact she was extremely disapproving about some of her friends' activities at college.

"I'm not sure Gina even tasted alcohol before she was in her early twenties. She was a mother to two children before she was even legally old enough to drink so it's no great surprise," remarked family friend Jim Huggins.

"Gina was a pretty straight shooter in those days. She hadn't done much in her life except have two kids and sit at home all day watchin' TV."

Gina was extremely devoted to babies Michael and Heather and she insisted on tending to both of them when they woke up in the middle of the night, even though Steve offered to help.

"Gina was a bit possessive about the kids. She said she didn't want Steve to get too tired because he had work to go to next day but it seemed like a bit of a controlling thing as well," observed Huggins.

Others who visited Gina's home at that time noted that everything was geared around herself and the two babies. Steve played second fiddle. Gina hardly ever talked about him. She just endlessly talked about herself and the babies and what they'd been doing.

Steve was working such long hours to make ends meet that by the time he got home he'd either flop in front of the TV or grab a beer and a plate of food and then fall into bed. The couple rarely went out together, partly because they couldn't afford it and partly because Gina didn't want to leave the babies with a sitter. She was particularly concerned about Heather, who had had a few breathing problems after she was born. Gina told Steve she preferred to be home nights to keep an eye on Heather.

Gina even used a baby monitor so she could hear if the infants woke up. She preferred to keep it on at all times.

Gina had a problem trusting people. Many of her friends and family put it down to her father's betrayal of her. And that betrayal continued to haunt her whenever her beloved Mother's Day came around on the second Sunday of every May.

TWO

Gina Hill had been greatly looking forward to Mother's Day 1986. She had two children, a loving husband and a long life of domestic bliss to look forward to. She was proud of achieving that after what her family had been through. Until she had traveled that road herself, she'd had no idea how hard it was being a mother.

Steve knew how much Mother's Day meant to his wife because she'd told him how she and her brother and sister celebrated it when they were children.

Mother's Day that year began with a card from Steve at the bedside:

> You've brought love and kindness into our life and you've loved me and your family. You've supported us in every way with your sharing and giving spirit.
>
> Thank You

Gina appreciated the effort he'd made and knew that he was preparing breakfast in bed for her as she blearily rubbed the sleep from her eyes and began to wake up properly.

When she heard baby son Michael calling for her a smile came to her face. She felt so lucky to have them all. Gina looked at her watch and was surprised it was so late. Heather usually woke her by 6 A.M. every morning. She'd turned the baby monitor off the previous night so that she and Steve could enjoy some uninterrupted love-making for a change.

The moment Gina walked into the children's bedroom she knew something was wrong. Michael was crying hysterically and looking in the direction of Heather's cot, where the tiny body was lying facedown. There was no sign of breathing. She looked stiff and lifeless.

Gina grabbed the infant and shook her desperately, then collapsed on the floor screaming her name over and over again.

"*Heather!*"
"*Heather!*"
"*Heather!*"

By the time paramedics turned up at the apartment it was too late.

Gina immediately plunged into deep remorse about Heather's death. She told friends and family that she felt she should have had Heather sleeping in her bedroom and kept a constant eye on her. She should never have turned that baby monitor off.

And the fact that it was Mother's Day simply compounded her emotional confusion.

"Gina was freaked out by it happening on Mother's Day," recalled her sister Jody. "That day had always been so important to us as a family. She blamed herself for Heather's death."

From then on Mother's Day took on new sinister connotations for Gina. She believed it was a doomed day.

And husband Steve did not—at least in Gina's eyes—provide the shoulder to cry on that she expected. "Problem was that Steve had been left out of things for so long that he found it real difficult to show emotion towards Gina," explained Jane Walsh. "Of course he cared for her, but he didn't know how to deal with it."

The funeral service for four-month-old Heather Hill was a grim affair consisting of just a handful of relatives and friends at a funeral home in Belleville just a short distance from the chapel where she and Steve had been married less than two years earlier.

Gina sobbed and husband Steve tried his hardest to console her. As her sister Jody pointed out: "It was a terrible, terrible day and I guess for Gina it was made even worse 'cause she knew she couldn't have another child."

As the tiny white coffin was carried into the funeral home by just one pall bearer, Gina turned away and stared into oblivion.

Back at home, everywhere Gina looked were reminders of her beloved daughter. For weeks after her death she couldn't even manage to cry herself to sleep at night.

Often she'd creep out of the couple's bed and slip into the kids' bedroom and sit on the floor and sob as she remembered how Heather would have been there.

Gina never forgave herself for her daughter's death. Her grief and guilt were further compounded by her having turned off the baby monitor to make love with husband Steve.

Gina was also haunted by her decision to be sterilized. She knew there was no turning back the clock. Nobody dared talk to her about it, but they all knew that she had made the biggest mistake of her life by getting sterilized.

Nothing could be the same again. She bravely told one friend that it wouldn't have mattered anyhow: she couldn't have re-created Heather, as there had only ever been one of her. Gina's friends and family knew when they talked to her that she was broken by the knowledge that she couldn't have any more children.

Yet Gina desperately needed to feel she could have another child because she believed that it was a vital part of any relationship. She also believed that if she could not have more children her husband would dump her.

Nothing could have been further from the mind of husband Steve. But that didn't stop it eating away at Gina. She became increasingly morose and bitter in the months following Heather's death. Her self-esteem dipped and she started binge eating at home while Steve was out at work.

Inevitably her weight ballooned and she became reclusive, only venturing out of the house at night because she didn't want the neighbors to see how much weight she'd put on.

Gina's state of severe depression manifested itself in huge rows with husband Steve when he got home exhausted after a hard day's work. Often Gina would storm out of the house and disappear for hours on end leaving Steve to look after Michael.

Eventually Gina's mom Sue stepped in and began spending more and more time caring for Michael because the family was so worried about the state of Gina's crumbling marriage.

Heather's death was like the spark that lit a fire of confusion for Gina. Her character reverted to a worse version of what it had been like before she met Steve. She looked on everyone as a threat to her happiness.

Instead of baking, cooking and keeping their home neat and tidy for her husband's return from work, Gina fell apart. The apartment fell into disrepair. She was often out when Steve got home at night. Their family and friends began speculating about when the couple would split up.

"It was only a matter of time. No couple could stay together through the sort of rows they were having," says friend Jim Huggins. "Steve tried to be understanding but he wasn't the sort of guy to put himself in someone else's shoes and although he knew why Gina had flipped he felt that she just needed to get everything back to the way it was."

But Gina Hill did not want it to go back to what it had been like before. Gina's master plan for happiness had crashed into a brick wall. It was a similar feeling for her as the day her beloved father walked out of the family home all those years earlier. Gina thought that maybe she was doomed to have a life peppered with disappointment, heartbreak and tragedy.

"Maybe I'm gettin' what I deserve but I don't want the life I had anymore. I gotta do something to change it," she informed Jane Walsh. Heather's death made her realize she had to look for something more in life. A feeling of being trapped in Belleville took over. She began desperately looking for a means of escape.

Not long afterwards the inevitable happened and Gina and Steve split up. Their two-and-a-half-year-old son Michael had been too young to fully appreciate his parents' unhappiness but some relatives insisted that he became withdrawn from the moment his baby sister died.

"You could see it in Michael's eyes. He was glazed and very unresponsive to questions. His learning abilities slowed right down for a while," said Jim Huggins. "We got no doubt that Gina's marriage problems and Heather's death contributed. He'd been caught right in the middle between those two fighting parents."

In many ways Michael was now the kid who was always in the firing line.

After the split with her husband, Gina moved back into her mom's house with Michael. Her family noticed an enormous change in her character and her social habits. She began going out to bars and clubs. She didn't seem interested in Michael. When her friends and family tried to confront her about it she got very defensive. A lot of them thought she was having a nervous breakdown.

Gina continued receiving some financial support from Steve to pay for Michael but instead of giving it to her mother to cover the cost of living in her house, she fell in with a crowd of old school friends.

For the first time in her life, Gina became a party

animal. Her mom was a built-in babysitter and those long, lonely daytime hours at home watching TV made Gina even more desperate to get out at night and see another side to life, something she'd never had time to do when she was a teenager.

As the weeks turned into months, Gina became virtually an absentee mother. "She'd be out 'til all hours and there were guys around her the whole time," recalled Jane Walsh. "She'd become a different person from the one I grew up with."

Gina hung out with a group of drop-outs at some of the seedier dives of Belleville—some of the very same taverns her father had frequented before his marriage split. Gina acquired a taste for alcohol for the first time in her life and began looking for men to date following the split from Steve, admitting to her friends that she needed a man with her at all times—and she wasn't that choosy.

The Pierce family couldn't help noticing that Gina was behaving in exactly the same way her father had. Gina had tried for years to fight against being like her father but now she was falling into exactly the same traps.

All this socializing soon began playing havoc with Gina's bank balance. She could not support her young son Michael and keep up the partying lifestyle. It was no surprise when Gina began bouncing checks all over Belleville in the company of "some bad-ass dudes" as her sister Jody later described them.

Soon the police were making regular visits to the Pierce house looking for Gina and her friends. There was even a warrant issued for her arrest. But Gina was never in when they came knocking.

Unknown to her family, Gina had fallen for an older man. The two had been sleeping together for some months when Gina dropped the bombshell that she was pregnant.

"Not only pregnant but that she was carrying twins," Jody later recalled. "Gina certainly didn't do things in halves.

"If we'd known she was goin' around saying she was pregnant we would've put them all straight."

Wanted for passing bad checks and "five months pregnant," Gina and her new love hot-footed it to Maryland. For a few weeks they completely disappeared and her family continued to deal with the Belleville police every time they came by the house looking for Gina.

Then Frank Posting made an angry phone call to Gina's mom and sister back in Belleville and her fantasy pregnancy was revealed.

"This guy called us up 'cause Gina had told him she'd had a miscarriage 'cause of all the stress we put her under," explained Jody.

"Well, we told him there and then that she couldn't even get pregnant. He was lost for words. Poor guy had been completely suckered by Gina."

Behind Gina's bizarre behavior lay a tragic attempt to sustain a romance by promising her man of the moment the ultimate prize: a child. As Jane Walsh later said: "It was as if she'd decided that she had to lie about bein' pregnant to keep her man and to control him. It was the only currency Gina knew how to spend."

Not surprisingly, Gina's romance with the older man fell apart shortly after she admitted to him that she'd made up the story about being pregnant.

Yet again, Gina returned to her mom's home in Belleville, sorted out her bad check problems and once more began vegetating at home while Michael started school and her mom went out to work to support them all.

But Gina needed a full-time man. It was her only means of survival and she couldn't stand being trapped at home for long.

THREE

In 1989 Gina Hill began dating a young serviceman from her home town. However, she soon noticed that his roommate was a much better prospect. It didn't take her long to switch affections.

Kevin Spann was a couple of years older than Gina and had two brothers and two sisters. He had been brought up in nearby Lebanon, Illinois. He'd joined the U.S. Army in his teens mainly because it was a tradition in his family.

Kevin was a quiet, reserved type of character. He'd graduated from college with a degree in electronics and was being trained by the U.S. Army as a telecommunications expert. He liked working with computers and was so good at math that he took numerous courses long after graduating. As Jody described him: "Kevin was one of those technical type of guys who always wanted to know how and why something worked."

Kevin Spann also happened to be a man of simple tastes. He didn't demand much of his fellow man. And his favorite hobby was collecting things—it didn't much matter what. As his father Harold later remarked: "If you made a card out of it he'd collect it."

Most of the time he kept his feelings to himself.

Jody recalled: "Kevin was a real nice, polite guy. The sort of person who wouldn't harm a fly.

"People thought he'd be like this tough-guy soldier type. But he wasn't interested in fighting. He was more involved in the electronics side of things. The guy loved gadgets, computers, you name it. He had one of them mechanical minds."

Many of Gina's friends back in Belleville were amazed at how quickly she managed to get herself a new boyfriend following the split with Steve and that Bonnie-and-Clyde romance with that older man. By this time she weighed almost 200 pounds, wore her mousy brown hair in an unmemorable medium-length style and tended towards baggy jeans and sneakers. Not exactly oozing with sensuality. At least not on the surface. But Gina's need for a man overcame all other obstacles.

"Basically, Gina couldn't survive without a man. She made that clear after she and Steve split up. She even admitted she wasn't happy unless there was a guy in her life. She used to say, 'fresher the better,' " recalled Jane Walsh.

Kevin Spann had just come out of a bruising long-term relationship with a local girl that had resulted in a pregnancy. But their split was so acrimonious that his old flame hadn't even informed Kevin she was pregnant. The truth only emerged many years later.

"Kevin had a lot of problems with that other girl," explained Jody. "She treated him real bad and kept running off back to her former boyfriend. Kevin got so upset that in the end he walked away from the relationship but if he'd hung around a bit longer he would have discovered that the girl was pregnant and would eventually have his baby."

Others who knew Kevin growing up in Illinois say that his response to that other girlfriend and the budding relationship between him and Gina was typical of his character.

"Kevin walked away from confrontations. He didn't want to know about certain things but he could put up with a lot of shit before he'd split from a girl," said one old friend, Nathan Blake.

"We used to tell him to stand up for himself but he was always afraid of the show-downs. It just wasn't part of his character. Trouble was a lot of the women in his life walked all over him."

By the time Kevin met Gina he'd already handed in his notice to the U.S. Army to pursue a new career. Kevin Spann was so electronically minded, he'd been assured he could double his income if he got into the computer business.

Gina was horrified when she heard that her new boyfriend was considering throwing away a safe, secure career and immediately set out to change his mind. Kevin even let slip that he could have taken up a posting to Germany if he'd stayed in the Army. Gina saw that as a perfect escape route from Illinois so it didn't take her long to persuade Kevin to change his mind about quitting.

She rapidly got Kevin Spann under her spell. Gina was adventurous in bed and she adored talking about almost any subject he was interested in. Kevin Spann had never met a woman like that before in his life and he was captivated.

Kevin became so transfixed by Gina that he was

soon prepared to do anything to keep her happy. In many ways he was similar to Gina's first husband Steve Hill.

It was almost as if Gina had to pick quiet types because she wanted to be in control. She certainly wasn't looking for a father figure.

Gina was going to hold on to this man even if it meant relying on one of her familiar plans to ensure he did not abandon her. She wasn't going to lose this one.

FOUR

"I got some great news, honey," Gina yelled into the telephone to Kevin Spann.

"I'm pregnant!"

There was a long pause at the other end of the line. Kevin was lost for words at the best of times but on this occasion he was completely dumfounded.

Gina had talked about having more children and how important it was for any loving couple. Kevin had wholeheartedly agreed with her when she asked him if he wanted children. He was keen to become a dad and had poured much love and affection in the direction of little Michael.

Gina had picked up on those signs and decided that she needed to hook Kevin Spann into her life permanently. She'd even researched the Army's pay scale and benefits and discovered that there was an associated benefit that paid extra dividends for the child of a serviceman even if that child was not his but his wife's. With ex-husband Steve Hill working in a lowly job, Gina knew there was little chance of him ever being able to afford to pay her enough to cover Michael's basic expenses.

Getting pregnant would be a brilliant way of setting herself up for a reasonably affluent life—or so Gina thought.

Kevin Spann had no idea that his girlfriend's pregnancy was imaginary. Why should he?

Kevin and Gina spent the following few weeks discussing babies' names, where they would live and even began looking in stores at baby clothes. Gina was delighted that Kevin seemed so excited by the prospect of fatherhood and she fed off that happiness by trying hard to make herself indispensable to him.

The truth about Gina's supposed pregnancy eventually came out in an incredibly hurtful manner.

Her sister Jody explained: "We got a call one day from Kevin's roommate saying that he'd just picked her and Kevin up from the hospital where she'd had a miscarriage. He said that Gina had said she'd lost the baby 'cause of the stress we'd put her under.

"Well, I just rolled my eyes. I couldn't believe that she was up to her old tricks again. I told the roommate that we should meet up 'cause I needed to tell him some home truths."

A few hours later Jody revealed the truth about Gina's pregnancy. "I let him know it was all a lie. He then told Kevin about it. He was pretty upset."

For the next few days Gina insisted to Kevin that her family was lying because they'd been jealous she'd gotten pregnant. She even claimed that she'd suffered physical abuse at the hands of her mother and sister.

Kevin was so confused about what had really happened that he called the hospital where he'd picked up Gina and asked them to confirm the miscarriage.

He discovered she hadn't even checked in to the medical center.

When Kevin finally plucked up the courage to confront Gina she confessed everything and begged for his forgiveness. She explained how Heather's death had affected her and an understandable wave of sympathy came over Kevin Spann.

Her sister Jody saw it in a entirely different light.

"Gina was the type of person who could wrap these kinda guys up, I guess," says Jody. "I don't know how she really did it. But I know she'd fill their heads with such crap and they'd get to feelin' sorry for her and start believin' everything she said."

Gina's obsession with always having a man in her life obviously came from not having a father with her throughout her childhood. But as old friend Jane Walsh explained: "Gina really needed a father-figure–type boyfriend or husband, not one of these quiet type of guys. I kept tellin' her to go for the noisy ones but ultimately she wanted to be in charge of any relationship. Guess she always wanted to be the one who decided when they left."

Gina's complex manipulation of her husband and lovers lay in the fear that history would repeat itself and she'd find herself alone in just the same way her mother had.

Gina had to be the one who made the big decisions, not the man she was involved with. These types of men were no threat and she happily used her sexual prowess to hold on to them.

Gina and Kevin Spann's courtship continued despite her phantom pregnancy. She told Kevin that what they both needed was a change of environment and the promised posting to Germany would be a perfect move for their relationship. Gina also continued to be impressed by the way Kevin treated her son, as if Michael were his own child.

However, Kevin remained reluctant to actually marry Gina and persuaded her to live with him in Lebanon. He was relieved when the posting to Germany was put on ice by the Army for a few months.

Kevin Spann didn't want to jump into a marriage following all those problems with his previous girlfriend. He also knew that once Gina became his wife she would qualify for a large share of his income. He even wondered if that was why she was so eager for them both to go to Germany.

"Gina didn't like the fact he wouldn't marry her straight away," explained her sister. "She wanted to have a piece of his money so she didn't have to work or nothin'. Gina was a very, very lazy person by this time. She would say she was sick all the time. That girl was sick more than anybody I know."

Gina's friends said that Kevin never realized how fake her bouts of "sickness" really were. He'd come home with takeout meals and beers and then proceed to wait on her even though he was the one who'd just been working.

Others saw this behavior as yet another form of controlling by Gina. And she continued to be extremely interested in Kevin's finances.

Once she'd seen young Michael off to school, Gina studied every minute detail of Kevin's insurance policies and pension plans, which she'd found in a drawer in their apartment. She even telephoned the company to clarify certain points.

Her quest to be secure for the rest of her life was of paramount importance. She never wanted to suffer the sort of financial embarrassments that had filled her painful childhood.

A couple of months after moving in together, Gina and Kevin drove over to nearby St. Louis to see some friends. During the thirty-minute drive Kevin mentioned to Gina that he'd been ordered to leave shortly to work a five-week stint at a training camp in Texas. Gina reacted by bursting into tears.

She couldn't bear the thought of spending time alone in Illinois. Gina was also extremely insecure about Kevin meeting other women while he was away. She'd already gotten into the habit of asking him at least ten times a day whether he loved her.

Kevin didn't know how to react. He wasn't interested in other women. And he genuinely didn't realize just how serious the situation was.

"Gina didn't like any man abandoning her even for that short a period of time," recalled Jody. Shades of what their father had done seemed to be ever-present in Gina's life.

In St. Louis, Gina laid her cards on the table. She told Kevin that unless he married her she couldn't guarantee that she would still be in Lebanon when he returned.

That afternoon they went to the nearest marriage office in St. Louis and made their relationship official. Gina had finally gotten her way.

Gina didn't even tell her son Michael that he had

a new father until they returned to Lebanon that evening. When Gina's sister and mom heard the news they just shrugged their shoulders. "Gina wanted a route out of Illinois and Kevin was there to provide it. We just hoped he knew what he was letting himself in for," recalled Jody.

Kevin's friends believe he was bulldozed into the marriage and were particularly perplexed that he would marry a woman who couldn't have any children.

But Kevin Spann seemed happy to be controlled and have his life organized by Gina, even if his lack of curiosity was extremely frustrating.

"Kevin was too gentle for his own good. We all told Gina she was damn lucky to have married such a decent man even if he was shy and quiet and didn't say much," explained her sister.

Just after their marriage, Kevin was told by his superiors that he'd have to do a one-year stint in Texas before being transferred to Europe. Kevin, Gina and Michael headed off to a base near Fort Worth.

At least Gina was escaping from Illinois. As close friend Jim Huggins explained: "The first we knew about her leaving was when she rang up from Texas. She sounded like a new person after all those earlier problems."

Down in Texas, Kevin and Gina seemed happy and content with each other. She felt more settled than ever before and she even tried to be more of a traditional home-maker.

The key to Gina's happiness was Kevin's presence in her life. Gina's few friends on the base soon noticed that she was very miserable whenever he was away. That's when all the old insecurities kicked in.

Gina was very good at torturing herself with jealousy about Kevin. She imagined him out at girlie bars or meeting other women even though most of his trips involved going to far-off places where there was a distinct lack of women on the agenda.

But she was about to get a whole lot lonelier.

FIVE

Gina Spann's plans for a life of leisure in Europe were rudely interrupted at 0200 local time on August 2, 1990, when Iraqi troops and armor rolled across the border to Kuwait. Kevin Spann and his fellow soldiers were immediately put on standby for war duty. He jealously watched as the first batch of soldiers packed their desert gear and departed for the Gulf.

Kevin was totally immersed in the wartime atmosphere and spent increasingly long hours at the base in Texas while Gina toiled at home in front of the TV.

By the end of August the U.S. and its allies were sending air and land forces into the Gulf at a rate of 20,000 troops a day.

At service bases across the U.S. the first thing noticed by visitors to the camps was the sheer magnitude and noise of the activity that was under way in preparation for war: vehicles revving, men shouting, helicopters hovering day and night.

Spann and his colleagues in Texas remained on a permanent state of readiness until their names were called. Saddam's invasion of Kuwait had the unexpected side-effect of seriously damaging Gina's hopes of domestic bliss. All her old feelings of insecurity and longing for another child kicked in.

Meanwhile Kevin Spann and his colleagues had their gear packed and ready. He'd even been careful to remember his Walkman, a shaving kit and a photo of Gina and Michael. He knew that if he found himself dumped in the middle of nowhere or hanging around a makeshift boot camp for months on end, that photo could prove his only lifeline.

Just before Christmas 1990, Kevin Spann finally headed for the Gulf, knowing full well that he would be unlikely to see Gina and Michael for a long time. Gina knew there was nothing she could do to stop him and for the first time since they met she wished she'd let him quit the Army and get a job in Silicon Valley.

She dreaded the long lonely nights and made it clear to Kevin that he'd better hurry up and return—otherwise she might not be there.

On January 16, 1991, with Iraq still refusing to withdraw from Kuwait, the UN Security Council authorized war and waves of U.S. and allied warplanes flew north.

The allied forces soon gained control of the air as they spent the next forty days and nights bombing and blasting Iraqi positions.

On February 24, the U.S. and its allies launched their ground war and Kevin Spann found himself heavily involved in telecommunications between forces. Within 100 hours the allies had broken what was left of Saddam's army and drove it from Kuwait.

Like many soldiers, Kevin Spann was not fully

aware of the risks he may have undertaken while in the Gulf. But he never forgot the ghastly oil fumes and the fear that diseases may have been spread by flies and other insects feeding off animal carcasses left to rot in the desert.

Then there had been the blaring alarms that were virtually a daily occurrence and sent troops scrambling for their gas masks and chemical suits—called Mission Oriented Protective Posture gear.

Kevin had been issued two of the charcoal-lined suits, which were supposed to provide protection from chemicals for seventy-two hours. But he and many others ended up wearing the same two suits for their entire tour of duty.

The only way Kevin Spann and his fellow troops knew if the air was filled with deadly gas was to watch the cats and wild dogs that wandered around his base in packs. "If they stayed alive then that told us there was no gas in the air. It was a crapshoot out there," said one soldier.

The Iraqis suffered an estimated 100,000 casualties and desertions ranged from 30 percent in some units to 60 percent in others.

In some ways it could have been a lot worse for Kevin. The U.S. and allied forces' overwhelming air superiority turned it into a one-sided battle before Spann and the other ground troops could properly get to work.

Staff Sergeant Kevin Spann realized within a short time after getting back to the U.S. that life would never be quite the same after the turmoil in Kuwait.

In the months following his return from the conflict

Kevin increasingly reflected on those subtle changes in his life.

He told one friend: "Everybody I know who was out there has changed some. They've got a different outlook on life. It means more to them now.

"You know, the green grass, the beautiful trees. There were no trees over there."

And Kevin reckoned he got out of the Gulf relatively unscathed compared with many of his buddies.

Ultimately he saw it as a year out of his life. He didn't know what the latest TV shows were. A lot of hit movies had just passed him by. But most important of all, what was his wife up to?

But Kevin Spann never once doubted the cause for which he was fighting. "He went into it as a soldier with a soldier's mentality. That was Kevin. His loyalty was unswerving," explained one Army friend.

Spann told other civilian friends that he felt duty-bound to join in the Persian Gulf conflict because of the way that countries like Iran and Iraq had treated the U.S. "We couldn't let 'em get away with it any longer," he told one relative. "At least by gettin' out there and doin' our thing we didn't get embarrassed like we did in the past."

Kevin Spann also noticed a change in the life inside the Army. Once the soldiers were completely allowed to stand down after the Gulf conflict, the service took on a flatter atmosphere.

"It was a difficult time because a lot of us were feeding off that adrenaline hit of bein' in a real live conflict. Now we were back and there wasn't a damned thing happening," explained Gulf War vet James Steen.

For Kevin Spann the choice was extremely clear. He could get out of the Army and struggle around looking for a computer job in what was by now a highly overcompetitive job market or he could stick with it and start training other soldiers.

He had experienced fighting a real war and wanted to pass all that on to other young soldiers. "You never know when they might have to be thrown in the deep end just like I was," he told one Army friend.

And that decision also sparked Kevin Spann's departure for Germany, much to Gina's delight.

She was excited by the prospect of leaving the U.S. while Kevin was more cautious about the entire move. He'd just spent almost a year abroad and he liked the creature comforts of home. He'd also heard a lot of stories about what bored servicemen's wives got up to on foreign postings.

SIX

Life in Germany proved a welcome relief to Gina and Kevin Spann for the first few months of the posting. Gina became friendly with a number of servicemen's wives and the couple began regularly entertaining other families at their on-base home.

She began to get out more, lost weight and started buying tighter-fitting clothes. It was all such a drastic change from the sneakers and jeans that she wore during endless wanderings around the shopping malls of Illinois and Texas.

She could reinvent herself in Germany and that made her far more confident about herself.

Gina was intrigued by the way the Europeans were more relaxed about many things—including sex. She told one friend at the time: "They're so much less uptight than back home. It makes everythin' better far as I'm concerned."

And Gina's interest in sex had never really diminished. Even in the dark days following the death of four-month-old Heather she needed to make love to her then-husband Steve, despite the emotional turmoil.

Meanwhile Kevin Spann remained more cautious,

some would even say unadventurous. He didn't like being drawn into conversations about such personal subjects and Gina found it all rather frustrating.

One quiet afternoon she dug out Kevin's servicemen's group life insurance policy. It said clearly that Gina and Kevin's stepson Michael would benefit to the amount of $200,000 in the event of Spann's death. It was nice to know that if anything happened to Kevin then she and Michael would be looked after.

Life in Germany provided an escape from all the irritations of the U.S. Gina had a definite spirit of adventure and she considered her stay in Europe to be an education. Whenever she tried to discuss this sort of thing with other servicemen and their wives, she got the strangest looks because not many of them gave such matters any thought.

In Germany, Gina's eye was caught by the openness of the sex clubs and brothels on the outskirts of most major towns, and by how everyone took it all for granted. She tried to explain this to Kevin but he just nodded his head slowly and tried to change the subject. He didn't really care for the Germans' attitudes towards sex.

Gina was disappointed that she'd married such a prude but she reckoned she was better off with a guy she knew all about than some dark horse who might be keeping secrets from her. That vein of insecurity which was sparked by her father's departure remained ever-present.

Gina encountered a few men during her trips to stores and movie theaters, often in the company of other servicemen's wives. Some of them noted that

Gina liked flirting with any reasonably handsome younger man she came into contact with.

But she never went any further because she genuinely wanted her marriage to Kevin Spann to thrive. She had a good lifestyle in Germany. She was more affluent than she'd ever been before in her life. Why throw it away?

In the middle of his posting to Germany, Kevin Spann had to return to the U.S. to attend Army school in South Carolina for four months in order to qualify as a training instructor. It was a dreadful blow to Gina. She tried to get Kevin to delay the exam until they returned full-time to the States, but Kevin told Gina he'd seriously damage his career if he didn't go.

Gina's response was intriguing. She had tried to stop his leaving because she didn't want to endanger her marriage, but once he defied her then her defenses went down and anything could happen after that. Friends and family believe Gina actually didn't trust herself and she feared that her appetite for men could prove very difficult to resist once Kevin was gone.

In fact Gina had already spotted a handsome young soldier who'd been working under her husband until his departure to the U.S. But she'd been so determined not to ruin her marriage that she'd kept well away from him. However once Kevin flew out she began thinking about the young serviceman again.

Michael Dunleavy was a polite, soft-spoken 24-year-old from Louisiana and he'd been entranced by Gina the moment their eyes met across a crowded dance floor during an Army dance a few weeks before Kevin set off for the U.S. They'd been introduced by

Kevin, who'd completely failed to notice the sparks that flew between them the moment they shook hands.

Within days of Kevin Spann's departure, Gina and Michael started dating. They went to the movies together, out for candle-lit dinners and even disappeared for three days to a hotel in Bavaria.

Although Gina didn't realize it herself, she was in a sense punishing her husband for daring to abandon her. She even admitted to one friend in Germany that she was surprised by how easy it was to switch affections to another man.

But then, she'd been educated for such a response since the day her father walked out on his family.

Gina's affair with Michael Dunleavy was soon the talk of the base. Many were surprised that the slightly plump housewife could attract such a handsome man.

"But Gina knew how to talk to these young guys and then once they got in bed with her they discovered things they never even knew about," one of her former lovers explained years later.

Gina treated each relationship as a genuine love affair. She professed her love for Michael shortly after first sleeping with him. She never saw herself as being promiscuous. She needed to be with a man and if one left her for whatever reason then she simply found another one.

Back in South Carolina, Kevin was studying hard, completely unaware of the domestic chaos occurring in Germany. Gina had conveniently put Kevin out of her mind and she was looking forward to the day when she would settle down with her new man. She seemed totally unaware of the consequences of her actions.

Gina even decided to ensure that her latest love did not escape her clutches.

Michael Dunleavy was just as shocked as his predecessors when Gina told him only two months after their affair had started that she was pregnant with his child. While Gina seemed positively glowing about the news, Michael feared that it could effectively end his Army career because of the strict rules that still existed about adultery within the service.

Gina's main concern was that she didn't want to run off with a man who was jobless. She assured Michael that no one need know about the pregnancy until the time was right. She was completely unaware that dozens of servicemen and their wives already knew about the illicit relationship.

For the next few weeks Gina and Michael spent virtually every available moment together.

Gina believed her "pregnancy" guaranteed that Michael Dunleavy would not abandon her. The couple even went down Gina's familiar route of looking at baby clothes and discussing names.

Gina had fine-tuned her pregnancy performance to the point where she knew the answer to everything. She'd already decided that, unlike last time, she wouldn't tell her man she'd had a miscarriage in a hospital. This time it would happen at home. She didn't want the same problems that she'd had before.

Then the inevitable happened: someone told Michael Dunleavy's commanding officer that he'd gotten Staff Sergeant Kevin Spann's wife pregnant. There was a double dose of disgust against Gina and her young lover because Spann was a Gulf War hero, a soldier who'd always gotten special respect wherever he went.

"All hell broke loose," explained Gina's sister Jody. "A lot of golden rules had been broken."

Kevin Spann got the inevitable phone call in South Carolina. He was stunned by the news and naturally concluded that Gina was up to her old tricks when he heard about the purported pregnancy.

Gina's family told Kevin to walk away from her. They reminded him about her behavior in the past and they tried to convince Kevin that this was a warning sign he should not ignore.

Typical of his character, Kevin refused to make a snap decision. He wanted to see how things panned out with Gina. He knew this other soldier would get blackballed out of the Army and he believed that the relationship would then end.

Kevin was desperate to hold the marriage together despite his in-laws' warnings. He remained convinced that young stepson Michael needed a strong family unit around him, and he still loved Gina despite all the chaos she had caused.

Back in Germany, Michael Dunleavy was hauled in front of his commanding officer where he confessed all and proudly announced that he intended to marry Gina as soon as her divorce came through. His pride about becoming a father was apparent to all who met him at the time.

A few days later, Michael Dunleavy was informed that he would be thrown out of the Army for "weight problems"—a convenient cover for the real reason, which was his admitted adultery with the wife of a senior officer.

Gina's sister and mother had seen it all before, although that did not make it any less staggering to hear about. "I couldn't believe she'd done it again," recalled Jody. "I realized that Gina was a very sick person who needed help. But I didn't know how anyone could deal with her."

What they didn't realize was that despite Gina's "record" of previous faked pregnancies she still had not revealed the truth to Michael Dunleavy.

Gina moved back to the U.S. just a few days after Michael Dunleavy. Kevin, who was still in South Carolina, was informed by her over the phone that when he returned to Germany she and son Michael would be gone. Kevin was heartbroken about losing the boy he considered to be his son. *And* he told Gina he still loved her.

Gina informed Kevin and the rest of her family that this time she had fallen for a man who really cared about her and she intended to marry Michael Dunleavy even though he was now discharged from the Army and living back at his parents' home in Louisiana.

Gina dropped her young son Michael at her mom's house in Belleville, headed straight for Louisiana and moved in with Dunleavy for what she told friends would be a lifelong relationship. Dunleavy's family still believed their son was about to become a father. Then Gina announced over breakfast one morning that she'd had a miscarriage.

Initial shock and sympathy for Gina was soon

overtaken by a deep-rooted suspicion that she was lying.

Eventually Dunleavy spoke to some old army colleagues back in Germany and was told about Gina's previous record.

Dunleavy confronted Gina about their lost "child." Instead of confessing, she screamed abuse at her young lover, then grabbed her bags and headed for the nearest Greyhound bus station.

Less than twenty-four hours later Gina turned up once more at the front door of her mom's house in Belleville, Illinois. It looked as if she would never completely escape from her dreaded family home.

For the following few weeks she made countless phone calls to Louisiana during which she professed her undying love for her young ex-soldier. Not surprisingly she then headed south, once again leaving young Michael in the capable hands of her mom. Gina told Sue Pierce and sister Jody that she expected to be married to Dunleavy before the year was out. How she'd managed to win him back again no one dared ask.

Gina even called Kevin in Germany and tortured him by telling him their marriage was definitely over even though she'd told him a few days earlier that they might be able to save it.

No one knows to this day if Gina really did go back to Louisiana because she quickly returned to her mom's house in Belleville. Crying hysterically, she claimed that this time it was over for good. Her mother and sister began to wonder if Gina could ever fix her life.

Caught in the middle of all this domestic chaos was seven-year-old Michael.

The Pierce family knew full well that the only truly familiar place Michael had known in his entire life was Belleville, Illinois. They made a point of telling Gina to leave him with them rather than take the child on any more of her pointless love jaunts across the globe.

Gina hated the idea of her son growing up in the very same house where she'd watched her parents' marriage break up but she had no money and little choice in the matter. In one way she was like any other parent: all she really wanted was a better life for her child than the one she had had.

Unfortunately she was managing to make it considerably worse.

Trapped in Belleville, without even enough money to go out with her old friends, it wasn't so surprising that life back with Kevin Spann began to seem a much more attractive alternative.

Kevin was one of the least vindictive people in the world. After what Gina had done to him most men would have been long gone. However Kevin Spann just wanted his life to get back to the way it was before they went to Germany.

During one of his many calls from Europe, Kevin informed Gina that he would be moving to Fort Gordon, near Augusta, Georgia, on his return from duty in Germany. She told Kevin to call her when he got to Georgia. Gina coldly informed friends that she'd probably join Kevin at Fort Gordon because it was her only route out of Belleville.

SEVEN

Fort Gordon was named after John Brown Gordon, a general from Georgia in Lee's Army of Northern Virginia and later a senator from Georgia. It covers more than 50,000 square miles of former farmland, including some of the most varied terrain in the South, which made it perfect for training soldiers in preparation for wars across the globe.

The fort itself was opened in 1941 to cope with the problems of troop training presented to the nation by the onset of the United States' involvement in World War II. At that time Camp Gordon, as it was known, was a one-purpose installation dealing only with the training of infantrymen and armored troops.

The fort housed three divisions that trained for action against Hitler: the Fourth Infantry (Ivy) Division, who were featured in Steven Spielberg's recent war epic *Saving Private Ryan* as some of the first soldiers to hit the Normandy beaches; the 26th (Yankee) Infantry Division; and the 10th Armored Division.

But when the world once again found peace in 1945, Fort Gordon turned into virtually a ghost camp and by the end of the forties the camp was run on only a standby status.

The Korean War brought new life to the fort and it was turned into a permanent military installation, which included a signal and military police school. In 1961 the U.S. Army Training Center was also set up to teach basic and advanced infantry and military police tactics.

The war in Vietnam once again breathed new life into the fort and all conflicts ever since have ironically done more than anything else to aid the survival of the compound.

During the Vietnam War, Fort Gordon even contained a Vietcong village for simulated training of soldiers. Some said it was so authentic you could smell death at twenty paces.

Inside Fort Gordon's strictly protected boundaries lay nearly 2,000 buildings, 100 miles of paved roads, ranges for small arms and artillery and numerous other facilities.

Throughout its history the troops stationed at Fort Gordon have always been expected—even encouraged—to join in the activities of the local civilian community. That was why Kevin Spann was encouraged to rent a house outside the fort's boundaries.

Senior officers inside Fort Gordon believe to this day that their open-door policy has led to far fewer problems at their military establishment than many others in the United States.

But the residents of Augusta didn't all necessarily agree.

In April 1995 Kevin Spann dropped back up to Belleville for what he hoped would be the last time and picked up Gina. It hadn't taken a lot of persuasion;

Gina needed to get away from Belleville and she knew that Kevin could look after her financially. Son Michael—now 11 years old—was left behind with his Aunt Jody because he needed to finish the school year. Jody promised to drive the child to Georgia the moment he finished school.

Yet again, Gina left Belleville hoping she'd never return. And Augusta sounded like a good place to live.

Certainly the U.S. Army had brought with it a massive infusion of military spending during the 1940s that changed Augusta forever.

With that had come a promise of $45 million to build a dam which would help supply electrical power to new industries in Augusta and bring power to farms, only 36 percent of which then had power.

By the time the 1950s came along Augusta was enjoying a classic post-revolutionary boom. The automobile and an era of cheap energy combined to produce enormous changes. The Gordon Highway cut through the heart of Augusta, the John C. Calhoun Expressway dumped traffic into the bustling downtown area of the city.

Paul Harvey, the famous radio commentator, once claimed that Augusta was the kind of place where men went to the barber shop to watch hair cuts. When he returned in 1963 he found that it had become "a thriving cosmopolitan metropolis filled with new industry."

But by the time Kevin and Gina Spann showed up in 1995 the city had done a complete about-face.

Out in the suburbs the automobile was forcing residences to spread farther and farther away from the city center. Cheap energy was reflected not only in where the houses were built but in how they were built.

Lower-middle-class districts filled with one-storey homes and, farther afield, trailer parks were developed at a rapid pace. Air conditioning lured people inside during the steamy Georgian nights and the television kept them there. The men who used to go to the barber shops to watch hair cuts now stayed indoors and watched wrestling on TV.

Back in downtown Augusta the only reminder of the good old days was the regular sight and sound of the freight trains blowing their horns at all times of the day and night. They shunted along the track that ran straight through the downtown area across numerous level crossings spread through the once thriving business district.

The only hope for Augusta's downtown area by the 1990s was that gasoline would skyrocket in price one day and bring the people back to the convenience stores and corner bars. The nearest Kevin Spann or any of his army buddies ever got to downtown Augusta was when some of the soldiers shot the breeze down at one of the half-dozen girlie bars that were the only businesses in the area capable of turning a profit.

By the mid-1990s some locals thought they could see some light at the end of the cloud of depression that had enveloped the city for so long. Local politicians insisted that population loss in the center had slowed down and a conscious decision was made to try and encourage folk back into the downtown area.

Developments along the Savannah River began emerging but the fact remained that families preferred the safety of the suburbs to the uncertainty of the narrow streets and shadowy alleyways of downtown Augusta once darkness fell.

What many of these families failed to appreciate, not just in Georgia but across the middle of America, was that once their children hit their teens there was absolutely nothing for them to do. Not allowed in bars until the age of 21, constantly warned to keep off the streets at night, it wasn't so surprising that those suburban kids began to get into all kinds of trouble.

It was also inevitable that the fast-food joints that flooded into the suburbs in the seventies and eighties would take the place of the friendly diners and the drive-ins of the fifties and sixties.

Kevin and Gina Spann found a home in the southeast corner of the city boundaries. Just nearby was a busy strip called Peach Orchard Road, a long, straight, messy collection of fast-food joints, cheap motels, car repair sites and the occasional clip-joint.

It had turned into the seedy underbelly of south Richmond County, where the Spanns had moved. Peach Orchard strip was a center for crime, drugs, prostitution and just about every other vice you care to name.

EIGHT

Like many servicemen who'd seen action, Kevin Spann was still finding it difficult to readjust to life back home and that made him especially anxious to get things back to the way they used to be.

Kevin had decided to make one last attempt to mend his marriage to Gina. Very few other men would have put up with her behavior but he insisted to family and friends that he saw a lot of good in her.

During Kevin Spann's phone conversations with Gina before she moved out of her mom's house, she had categorically stated that she wanted certain things if they were going to get back together—even though he was the one doing her the favor. Those conditions included a decent-sized house, a car apiece and payment for all of Michael's requirements, including food and toys.

Kevin agreed because he was so eager to save the marriage. But in the back of his mind he was extremely worried about how he could possibly afford all these extra expenses. His Army salary barely covered the cost of the rent on the house she was demanding, so Kevin knew he'd have to get some other work to keep things afloat. One or even two part-time jobs meant working all hours of the day and night, leaving Gina and Michael to look after themselves. But Kevin decided it was worth it if it helped save his marriage.

Even though the Gulf War had been over for four years there were still constant reminders of the conflict everywhere that Kevin Spann turned.

He particularly noticed that the health of some of his colleagues just wasn't the same as when they left for the Gulf in 1990.

A lot of them had what could only be described as semi-permanent flu but without the actual fever. Little infections kept popping up all over the place.

At first Kevin refused to concede that those semi-permanent ailments might be linked to exposure to certain chemicals in the Gulf.

But then the Army itself began admitting that there had been dangerous exposure to fallout from the bombing of Iraqi chemical and biological warfare plants and bunkers. Those soldiers who had been exposed ran a high risk of suffering from what had become known as Gulf War syndrome. Some troops had picked up mystery viruses which seemed to be a reaction to a nerve agent pretreatment drug that all U.S. troops received to protect them from Iraqi gas attacks. There was also the risk that illness could be picked up from contact with Iraqi prisoners.

By 1996, about 53,000 men and women who had served in the Gulf had reported symptoms of so-called Gulf War syndrome.

Inside Kevin Spann's base at Fort Gordon, physicians at the Dwight D. Eisenhower Army Medical

Center were still seeing six Gulf patients a week up
until the end of 1996.

Kevin Spann discussed the Gulf War syndrome
problem extensively with his family. He was particularly concerned by reports that exposure in the Gulf
had been blamed for infertility problems and birth defects. He still desperately wanted a child of his own
and during his problems with Gina he'd seriously
considered what he'd do if they did break up. He was
well aware of Gina's phantom pregnancies and that
she could no longer have children—and she kept
proving to him that it was dangerous to look to the
long term when it came to their marriage.

When Kevin Spann mentioned his worries about
infertility to Gina she took it very personally. Gina
even accused Kevin of hurting young Michael's feelings by making it so obvious that he wanted a child
of his own. Kevin was very upset by that suggestion
but, as was so often the case, he did not fully explain
his feelings to anyone, let alone his own wife.

Kevin had a classic soldier's mentality towards
talking openly about personal matters. He didn't see
it as his duty to be talking on such terms with anyone.
He'd been taught not to ask awkward questions and
that deadened the need to be curious.

It certainly built a barrier between himself and
Gina when it came to discussing sex, children, money
and most of the things that young couples need to
communicate about.

Meanwhile Gulf War experts were publicly pro-
claiming that twenty-one different substances from
the Gulf, including pesticides and oil, could cause infertility, miscarriage or birth defects.

In Florida, the Association of Birth Defect Children documented fifteen cases of Goldenhar Syndrome among the children of 283 Gulf veterans. This rare birth defect, characterized by asymmetrical faces and ear defects, normally affected one in 20,000 children.

The more Kevin Spann heard about this the more unsettled he became. He had a bad feeling about Gina even though they were stumbling on together. Now worries about his own health and ability to father children were making their relationship even more precarious.

NINE

Kevin's increasing obsession with having children of his own had a very ominous side-effect on Gina. Her self-esteem dipped alarmingly and she began binge eating at their newly rented house in Augusta while Kevin was out holding down three jobs at the same time.

Gina felt like a failure even though Kevin Spann tried in his own undemonstrative way to reassure her that this was not the case.

She also continued to feel enormous guilt about the death of baby daughter Heather and her decision to be sterilized. When Mother's Day came around each year she would retreat into a world of self-denial about what had happened. She even tried to completely ignore that celebration.

Caught in the middle of all this was her son Michael, who was confused by his mother's refusal to celebrate what was supposed to be a happy day. But that anniversary ate away at Gina's conscience. She just could not forget what had happened.

Gina increasingly resented the way Kevin would not properly discuss certain issues even though they both knew about the underlying problems that existed between them.

"Once again, Kevin was doing his burying-his-head-in-the-sand routine," said Gina's friend Jane Walsh. "It was his way of dealing with it but it was frustrating the hell out of Gina."

Kevin had bought his wife an almost new Chevy Cavalier convertible and rented a reasonable-sized house that he could ill afford—and, as usual, he was very concerned about the welfare of Gina's son Michael. He felt that should have been enough to offset the emotional roller coaster that Gina seemed to be riding. But in the spring of 1996 the atmosphere in the house in Augusta began to deteriorate. By early summer it got so bad that Gina informed Kevin she was moving back up to her family's home in Illinois to give herself some time to work out their future.

Kevin was shocked by her decision. But, as was so often the case, he didn't fully communicate his feelings on the subject and Gina headed north with son Michael not really knowing where she stood.

Running away had become an automatic reaction to any marital difficulties for Gina. She kept saying how much she hated life back in Belleville but when it came to the crunch it was the one place she went.

Many of Kevin's Army friends said he was well rid of Gina. But Kevin didn't see it that way. He still wanted to save the marriage despite all the past problems. At least there didn't seem to be another man involved this time.

Back in Belleville, Gina found herself a single parent once again. She became extremely withdrawn and began spending much of the daytime on the family's computer, which was connected to the Internet. She took the attitude that it was better than binge eating, which seemed about the only alternative during Michael's school hours.

Soon Gina was expertly surfing the net. It was the first time since junior high school that she'd actually had to put much thought into anything and she immensely enjoyed working at that computer. She joined a number of chatlines during those long, lonely hours spent at home in the daytime, and began communicating with a number of men. She carefully constructed some personal history about herself and wrote in such a clear and concise manner that numerous men were soon lining up for chats. Her attention was soon caught by one young netter named Jesse who was extremely responsive towards her lengthy e-mails.

Gina never told her sister and mom that she was using their computer to try and fix up a new relationship. But Gina reckoned it all made perfect, logical sense. She didn't have the money to go out bar-hopping to find a man, so why not do it on the Internet for the cost of a local phone call?

Over in West Virgina, teenager Jesse Dunn couldn't believe his luck. He seemed to have captured the heart of a fantastic-sounding lady who was keen for them to meet up one day.

Gina always claimed that she hadn't been looking for love when she placed an on-line message asking for pen pals. So adamant was she that she pressed home the point with capital letters.

Within a week however, Gina and Jesse were e-mailing each other every day. By the end of the second week, it was several times a day.

Their relationship grew intense—even though they

hadn't even spoken to each other at that stage. That was when the flirting began. She would say something outrageous and then follow it quickly by saying: "Hope that don't offend you."

Gina the natural flirt was in her element on the Internet. Soon the couple were talking dirty by describing what they'd like to do to each other.

During that early stage of their Internet romance, Gina hinted at her domestic problems by coldly cataloguing all the abuse she claimed her husband "Sandy" had inflicted on her. The way she wrote the information made it sound more like a police report.

Throughout those early communications Gina resisted the temptation to give out Kevin's real name. She just kept subtly mentioning how brutal and heartless "Sandy" had been to her and that she was looking for a means of escape from her appalling marriage.

Gina's conversion to computer literacy turned staying back in Belleville into a much more pleasant experience. She told friends she was enjoying it more than at any other time, including her childhood.

In the middle of all this, Kevin Spann began regularly phoning Gina in Belleville and suggesting she travel back to Augusta so they could try and save their marriage. Gina was sorely tempted but decided to keep Kevin at arm's length while she developed her relationship with her new, young Internet friend.

As that friendship with Jesse progressed she would occasionally test out other men older than Jesse. She loved the fact that she could do this without actually having to meet them. But Gina rapidly concluded that Jesse was the best bet. He was a clean-living, nondrinking kid with a lot of interests similar to hers. The sexual acts she described to him sounded out of this world to the impressionable youngster.

When Mother's Day 1996 was on the horizon in the last week of April, Gina began to get terrible nightmares of the kind she so often had suffered since her daughter Heather's death ten years earlier. But this time they seemed even worse. She went to a local doctor and was prescribed antidepressants to help her cope with the strain.

Gina felt unable to turn to anyone apart from Jesse on the Internet to explain the complexities of her feelings. Kevin's only interest was in mending his marriage. Mother's Day just didn't strike a chord with him.

Gina felt increasingly isolated as Mother's Day approached. To compound her feelings she was living back at her mom's house in Belleville where the family had disintegrated following her father's walkout.

On Mother's Day itself, Gina escaped the celebrations by slipping upstairs to the family computer. Within minutes she was locked into a heavy chatline conversation with Jesse. She told him that it was time to meet and she gave him her phone number and address. It seemed a very therapeutic way of dealing with the twisted emotions of Mother's Day.

Benjamin Michael "Jesse" Dunn was born on July 6, 1976, and still lived with his parents in West Virginia when Gina entered his life. An unlikely participant in the chaotic life of Gina Spann, thanks to the wonders of the Internet, he found himself involved in a love triangle that most teenage boys can only dream about.

Jesse was, like many teenagers, feeling bored with life. But never in a million years did he imagine he would have a relationship with a 30-year-old housewife from Augusta. He had been instantly entranced by the highly eloquent messages sent by Gina, who admitted she was married, but said that it was a dead relationship and that she was looking for a little excitement.

Young Jesse Dunn was convinced that Gina was a genuine woman and he liked the fact that she seemed so open about herself and her problems. He was extremely inexperienced and she sounded like someone who could really teach him a lot.

On Memorial Day weekend of 1996, Gina drove up to West Virginia in the dark blue convertible Chevy Cavalier bought for her by husband Kevin and checked into a motel near Jesse Dunn's parents' home with the express intention of starting an affair with the 19-year-old.

As one of his friends pointed out: "She was like his mom from the moment they got together. She was in charge. She liked it that way."

Jesse was not particularly sexually experienced and found himself completely swept up by Gina and her uninhibited ways.

After five days, most of which were spent in bed together, Gina announced to the lovestruck teenager that she was planning to move back to Georgia and she wanted him to join her. They set off together that same day.

On the way Gina told Jesse she was having problems with her husband and they would be living in a small rented place in an area called Grovetown while she tried to end her marriage.

Gina repeated to her young lover that she'd split with her husband because he'd been beating and abusing her. "I felt real sorry for her," Jesse later recalled.

Meanwhile, Kevin Spann, blissfully unaware of his estranged wife's promiscuous behavior, still wanted to save their marriage. The fact that he was even trying continued to be a source of amazement to his family and friends.

Gina's biggest problem had been how she could survive without Kevin's money. She told Kevin that she'd move back to the Augusta area for one month and see how things progressed. But she would not move back in with Kevin—he had to rent her a cottage while they saw how things went. Obviously, he had no idea that she was planning to share it with her teenage lover.

At first Jesse Dunn felt completely at home with Gina in their little two-bedroom house in an area called Grovetown. For an entire month Gina kept her young lover in the cottage rented by her husband without Kevin Spann ever realizing that he was financing her sex life.

One night Gina slipped out of the cottage for a rare night out with Kevin. The couple had an argument that culminated in Gina screaming at Kevin that their marriage might be savable if they could move to a better house than the "dump" they'd had before her last departure for Belleville.

Kevin was so shaken by the quarrel that the next

day he headed out to the nearest real estate broker and found a large three-bedroom house on Old Waynesboro Road on the southeast side of Augusta, in south Richmond County. He'd just been promoted to a supervisor in Company D of Signal Battalion 442 at Fort Gordon. But the small amount of extra income would be instantly swallowed up by Gina's expensive tastes.

Kevin Spann genuinely believed that if Gina felt more settled they might be able to rekindle their marriage.

"But, honey, does it have a pool?" asked Gina when Kevin rang her with the news about the new house. She was well aware that while she had Kevin in this sort of conciliatory mood she might as well get everything she wanted.

Kevin Spann hesitated. He so wanted to make Gina happy. "Nope. But I'll tell you what. I'll buy you one when my next income tax refund comes in."

Gina wondered how long that would be. But she had already decided to hatch an outrageous plan that most wives would not even consider, let alone carry out.

Gina moved her young lover into the new house while Kevin Spann was out at work. Jesse had no job at the time, so he knew he had to stick close to Gina if he was going to survive. And she only had a small income from her husband as far as he could tell. She kept telling him she needed a job.

Gina was scheming to make sure she did not lose that income support money from the Army. She later claimed she'd casually mentioned to Jesse that her husband Kevin was going to be in the house as well. But Jesse says he never heard her.

"When I got there and realized her husband would be in the house too I felt I'd been deceived by Gina," he later recalled. Jesse soon began to realize that she'd been lying about a lot of other things, too. For the following few days, Gina managed to keep her young lover and husband apart so that Kevin had no idea Jesse was her bedmate. Then she decided she needed to disappear with Jesse for a few days to try and figure out how she could make the arrangement work.

In the middle of all this, Gina's sister Jody showed up in Georgia with young Michael, who'd been at school up in Belleville.

Jody immediately sensed there were problems. She had been waiting for more than an hour outside the house when Kevin Spann turned up looking extremely agitated.

He told Jody he had no idea where Gina was. "She dropped me off at the base three days ago and I haven't seen her or the car since."

Jody's conclusion was predictable. "I thought, 'Here we go again.' " She then went into the house with Kevin and started calling around to try and track down her sister. Her mother said that Gina had just been on the phone to her and told her that she had a 19-year-old boyfriend named Jesse Dunn.

"When I heard that, I got the hell outta there. I just couldn't take any more of this shit that Gina was causing," Jody later recalled.

TEN

Kevin Spann was stunned when he eventually discovered from Jody that Gina had moved her young lover into the new house. When Gina returned from her three-day stay at a motel with Jesse Dunn, Kevin demanded a divorce. This time, he told her, he meant it, even though he hated having to deal with the issue.

But Gina told her husband she had no other place to go and announced that she wanted to continue living with her new lover and estranged husband under the same roof.

Most husbands would have rejected the proposal as ludicrous, but Kevin Spann hated any confrontations and mumbled an agreement. It was the biggest mistake he would ever make.

Meanwhile a bemused Jesse Dunn was confused by his status within the household. After all, he'd only just found out Gina's husband's name was Kevin—not "Sandy" as Gina had been telling him for months over the Internet. Jesse began to wonder how many other lies he'd been told by Gina.

"This whole big thing about her lying and, and her not lying anymore and being straight with me and everything. She was, as far as I can tell, she was a compulsive liar. She was lying about everything basically," Jesse later recalled.

"There were so many lies I can't even begin to, just about every word that came out of her mouth was a lie. And most of it involved Kevin, most like, this is what I can gather."

Gina Spann believed she could get through the complex domestic arrangement by creating a psychological barrier between her husband and young lover. She certainly did not want them forming a civilized relationship.

"She kept telling me that he abused her. Physically. He physically abused her," Jesse recalled.

Gina told her young lover that Kevin was a brutal bully and she was too scared to be alone with him. She claimed that no one would mind Jesse living with her in the house because he was in a sense protecting her from Kevin. She also insisted that she did not sleep with Kevin anymore so there would be no problem in that direction, either. Jesse Dunn remained confused. But he did not have much choice.

Neighbors on Old Waynesboro Road had little idea of what was happening inside number 3805. The house had only recently been rented out so no one knew the precise complexities of the relationships behind its closed doors.

Gina continued hammering home the message to Jesse that her husband was a wife-beater even as they lay together in a double bed that had been set up in the main living room area of the house. Kevin and Gina's son Michael had their own bedrooms at the back of the property.

But Jesse Dunn was puzzled by the fact that there were no marks whatsoever on her body. "I never saw any bruises. I never saw any marks. So I was starting to get real suspicious about the stories she was telling."

Meanwhile Jesse and Kevin gradually adjusted to putting up with each other being in the house. They avoided talking or any confrontations for the sake of Gina's son Michael. Jesse began to wonder if Kevin Spann was really the brutal wife-beater Gina had portrayed. "He never seemed to be any, like, like as mean as she made him out to be."

Gradually, they even started talking to each other.

"It just seemed that he was in a situation that, you know, he was a soldier and she was his wife and he really couldn't get out of it, you know."

Gina told Jesse that her husband was obliged to make a monthly payment to her and that was the other reason why she couldn't leave the house. She also admitted she was worried that if he got transferred to another base their marriage would end and she'd be left with nothing.

It was only some months later that Jesse actually began to realize the significance of what she was saying.

About two months after moving into the new house, Gina did something that amazed her family back in Illinois: She got a job working at a Hardee's fast-food restaurant on Washington Avenue, close to the busy Augusta National Freeway.

However, Gina immediately clashed with a couple of members of staff and quickly moved to another similar job at a nearby Taco Bell, at 25 Peach Orchard Road—the notorious local strip that had become a magnet for every bored teenager and lowlife for miles around.

She confidently informed Jesse she expected to be rapidly promoted once she settled in at Taco Bell.

Jesse couldn't help but be impressed by Gina's overt confidence. "She was a good talker and she made you feel like you were real special," he recalled. "I knew she was dishonest in many ways, but I didn't want to truly believe it. There seemed to be some real goodness somewhere inside her."

There was certainly a soft side to Gina that was rarely exposed in public. Jesse and many of the other men in her life insisted she was attentive, loving and extremely loyal to her man-of-the-moment. Jesse noticed how knowledgeable Gina was and the fluent way she lured him into a relationship through the Internet. But then, she had spent the previous ten years alone with her thoughts while her man was out at work. She didn't read many books but her curiosity was fueled by her vast appetite for glossy magazines and tabloids. "Gina was what I'd call book smart, definitely book smart," said Jesse some years later.

That so-called "book smartness" would soon make Gina popular with many of the younger staff members at Taco Bell. She saw her new job as an excuse to begin a new chapter in her life.

ELEVEN

Taco Bell was proud of the fact that in 1996 its sales ballooned to $5 billion dollars thanks to people's addiction to their fast foods.

The world's largest quick-service Mexican-style restaurant chain even managed a profit of almost $1 billion. More than 55 million people visited a Taco Bell restaurant in any given week in the U.S. and over 4.5 million tacos were sold each day in those restaurants.

Taco Bell employed more than 100,000 people throughout the U.S. and half the nation's population saw a Taco Bell commercial in 1996 at least once a week.

All new employees were told in no uncertain terms that Taco Bell's corporate culture was based around a fast-paced, dynamic, progressive company that believed constant change was healthy for staff. The company was also immensely proud that all their registers rang at every store.

By 1996 Taco Bell had became the favorite hangout for many of the bored youth on the Peach Orchard strip in south Richmond County.

It was inevitable since many of those very same youths had part-time jobs at the restaurant so their friends often stopped by.

Taco Bell on the Peach Orchard strip had become a particular meeting point for truant kids from the two local high schools, Butler and Hephzibah. In Richmond County thousands of high school students were given in-school suspension for cutting classes each year.

One of the biggest problems facing students at both Butler and Hephzibah was gross overcrowding in the classrooms. Enrollments kept rising, cramming more students into buildings designed to hold hundreds less.

Some students at Hephzibah had even been forced to take classes in the school gym and lunchroom because the student population outnumbered the available classrooms.

As one student said: "It's no wonder a lot of students cut school if they can. It's a hell of a problem."

Ditching school was often a spontaneous move by teenagers, which meant they needed somewhere to hang out. And that Taco Bell on the Peach Orchard strip was the perfect place to keep out of sight.

Eighteen-year-old Butler High student Jason Swallow had been working at Taco Bell on Peach Orchard for a year and a half when Gina Spann joined the staff.

"At first she was just one of the older ladies. You know those home-maker types lookin' for somethin' to do while their old man is out at work?" he later recalled. "I didn't know her that well at first. She looked kinda typical. A bit fat, but she seemed a lot cooler than many of the older people who worked there. She didn't look down her nose at us if you know what I mean."

Jason was impressed because Gina didn't take any notice of the age barriers between her and many of the other workers at Taco Bell. "She preferred hanging out with me and a couple of the other guys working there. We'd share a cup of coffee at break-time and talk about a lot about a lot of things, you know."

Gina took a genuine interest in the boys' lives—something that Jason and the others were not used to. "I was gettin' real shit at home at the time and just to talk to someone older seemed kinda weird. I didn't think anyone over twenty-five would understand what it was like to grow up in a place like Augusta."

But Gina knew the feeling. The Peach Orchard strip and the surrounding streets weren't that different from the wrong end of Belleville where she grew up.

Jason introduced Gina to some of the other regulars at Taco Bell who'd turned the fast-food joint into such a well-known hang-out for local teenagers.

Jason recounted: "A few of my old buddies from Butler High would come and shoot the breeze. We'd give 'em free coffee and cookies."

One of those youths was Chris Bargeron, an overweight 16-year-old with a reputation for skinning pet hamsters and playing tasteless jokes on his classmates at Butler High.

Bargeron was a quiet, reserved character who would occasionally explode into a stream of cutting observations about the people around him. But many of his contemporaries were weary of Bargeron.

"He looked much older than sixteen and talked like he was in his twenties. Chris didn't miss a trick but 'cause he looked kinda dumb a lot of people took no notice of him," explained Jason.

"I went to Butler High with him. He was a regular guy at the Taco Bell. But Chris could be real weird. At school he, like, tortured animals and stuff. Don't reckon he changed much when he started cuttin' school," added Jason.

Gina Spann didn't take a particular shine to Chris Bargeron because of his bulky physique and the fact that he seemed a bit weird. But she would eventually have a reason never to forget him.

During those early days at Taco Bell, Jason Swallow's conversations with Gina rarely covered the subject of her marriage. "It was real obvious that they didn't, like, have a relationship anymore," recalled Jason. "But I didn't like to ask any personal questions. Reckoned it was none of my business."

Jason was surprised when a youth named Jesse turned up at Taco Bell one day and introduced himself as Gina's boyfriend.

"I'd thought she was married and all. She never told me how it all worked out at home with Jesse and her husband. I guess what someone does in their life is up to them.

"But Jesse was a cool guy, pretty near the same age as us. We got talking to him and Gina one day and I asked them how they met since he was from outta town and all that."

"We met through the Internet," laughed Gina as she squeezed her young lover's hand. Jason and the others who were sitting around a table in the back storeroom at Taco Bell nodded their heads with approval.

Explained Jason: "A lot of my buddies got together

with girls on the Internet. You're stuck in a dead-end town like this where there ain't many places to hang out, you gotta meet girls somehow, haven't you?

"It's no different from a blind date, is it? Gina reckoned it was better 'cause you had a chance to get to know them before you dated them."

Jason added: "Guess you'd call it cyberlove. Seemed kinda cool to the rest of us. At least they seemed really in love."

During one of his many coffee breaks with Gina, Jason and his friends talked about how bored they were with their lives. Gina nodded her head in agreement.

"I missed out on a lotta that kind of thing myself 'cause I married and had kids so young," she told her young friends. Then with a smile she added: "Hey, how 'bout we all go out one night? I'll drive."

"Cool," came Jason Swallow's reply. Anyone with a car was worth their weight in gold to the teenagers at Taco Bell.

A few days later Gina Spann drove Jason and two friends into downtown Augusta and they ended up in a spit 'n' sawdust tavern on one of the old-style blocks that lined the wrong side of the tracks. "At least they didn't give us any heavy shit about our age, 'cause we had Gina with us," related Jason. Gina then began asking Jason and his friends some very specific questions about a subject that the youths had become extremely cautious about.

"She wanted drugs and stuff. I was kinda surprised at first 'cause she was, you know, older than us and we thought she was kinda square."

Jason and his friends were reluctant to be drawn

out on such a sensitive issue. "We'd been at a school where the drug enforcement cop came onto campus once a week to tell us how to inform on kids doing drugs, so when this older women starts askin' we were a bit freaked out."

Gina assured her new young friends that she was genuinely interested in doing drugs. However it was clear to the boys that she didn't know much about them. Jason explained: "She kept referring to 'marijuana,' rather than 'weed' and she seemed kinda nervous about it. But she didn't make us feel trashy like a lotta older people, so we decided to do some partying with her."

Gina Spann knew all along that these new friends of hers would find her some drugs.

At first glance Jason Swallow appeared fairly healthy. His eyes weren't bloodshot, at least no more than those of a typical teen suffering from too little sleep. But each day Swallow and some of his old friends from Butler High School smoked marijuana before, then after, work, and at school and always late at night.

"It cooled me off. It chilled me out," explained one Butler student when asked about his drug-smoking habits.

At Taco Bell some of the employees would smoke marijuana out in the back yard during breaks. "It sure helped pass the time and we had some real funny times," explained Jason.

Over the following few weeks, Gina Spann more than made up for her reluctance to take drugs during her own lost youth.

On a series of wild nights out with Jason Swallow

and some of the other youths who frequented Taco Bell, she smoked cannabis, snorted cocaine and amphetamines and even smoked some crack.

As Gina continued partying with her new friends, her young lover Jesse Dunn became increasingly unenthusiastic about her newfound obsession with taking drugs and having a good time.

"I went along with her a lot of the time but I felt kinda out of place 'cause I didn't do much of that stuff," he later explained.

The older staff members at Taco Bell treated Gina Spann with a lot of suspicion. "They didn't like the way she was hanging 'round with us. It made them kinda suspicious about her motives but none of us cared," recalled Jason Swallow.

The Taco Bell teenagers started treating Gina as if she was one of them. She'd organize their social lives and they all enjoyed her company. And most importantly, she had a car.

Jason was convinced that Gina was making up for missing out on all the drink and drugs she didn't take as a teenager.

"She used to say she'd had a boring life until she got to Taco Bell. Kinda weird to think that hanging out at Taco Bell was the highlight of somebody's life, ain't it?"

Then Gina was introduced to another, even more notorious drug—LSD.

LSD—or d-lysergic acid diethylamide-25 to give it its full name—is capable of producing profound and unusual psychological changes. And it was the drug that Gina Spann was most interested in.

LSD increases the electrical activity of the brain, and scientists say that its short-term psychological effects include overt mental activity.

When Gina Spann first took acid, she immediately reveled in the way the drug distorted her perception of space and time. Colors became greatly intensified; perceptions fused so that sounds were seen and colors heard.

Lucid thoughts rushed through her mind. It was almost as if she were creating a psychosis on a short-term basis. She didn't see it quite like that, though. To Gina Spann, she was "expanding her mind."

But by taking acid on numerous occasions there can be little doubt that she would have succumbed to what scientists call a "regression to more basic types of psychological functioning." Her defense mechanisms and ability to recall certain events would have been impaired, meaning that she was becoming more and more dependent on those around her who were also taking the drug.

Her friend Jason Swallow remembers those LSD trips vividly.

"Wow, they were weird trips, but I never felt uncomfortable with her and Jesse. We had that kinda friendship thing between us and we got on real well at that time."

Jason recalled one occasion when Gina agreed to drive four boys into Augusta after they each dropped an LSD microdot.

"We told her it was kinda crazy to drive on acid, but she insisted. It was almost like she felt responsible for getting us home and therefore had to drive.

"Turned out to be the coolest drive I ever been on. The trees seemed to come alive and every car that passed us looked like it had a blue light on top of it. And the signals at each stop light kept flashing the weirdest colors.

"But, you know, throughout that drive Gina just laughed and laughed. And she got us downtown without any problems. We ended up in some bar on the wrong side of the tracks, but Gina looked after us. It was a cool evening."

Gina Spann had become her young friends' designated driver. It didn't matter how much weed, acid, crack or booze she'd had. Gina would still get them all home like the mother figure she truly was.

Back at the house on Old Waynesboro Road, Gina continued sleeping with Jesse in the front room while her husband and son had their separate bedrooms at the back.

Gina frequently brought up the subject of her brutal husband whenever she was alone with Jesse. One day she got so emotional about what she claimed he was doing to her that she begged Jesse to help her kill Kevin. Jesse thought she was joking at first. When it became clear she was not, he changed the subject.

A few days later Gina produced a video camera and insisted that Jesse allow her to film them making love in the house. Jesse readily agreed.

Gina carefully set the camera up and switched it on and then returned to their bed where every position and sexual activity was recorded. Over the following few months Gina regularly used the video to enhance her sexual activities with her young lover. She liked to play back certain sequences as they made love in front of the TV with the VCR connected.

Gina also introduced another element to those encounters. She began talking about her own sexual fantasies, some of which involved killing her husband. She got so excited by talking about this that it often brought her to a climax before her young lover had even penetrated her.

One day Gina was out in her car with Jesse and started talking about killing Kevin. She tried to use it as a kind of turn-on, even though Jesse was desperately trying to avoid the subject.

Then she produced her home video camera once again and insisted that Jesse film her driving.

That video started with footage of a fat, black fly perched on a car wing mirror. Then Jesse could be heard saying: "We're movin' up to the forty-five-miles an hour level." The words could just be made out.

Then Jesse began referring to what Gina wanted to hear about: Kevin's murder.

"Man down . . . gunshot wounds . . ." Jesse was impersonating a police radio call-out on the shooting of Kevin Spann.

Those words, "gunshot wounds," were Gina's cue to come on screen. Her hair was in a neat bob cut and she was wearing shades.

"A cannon. Bye . . ." Her laugh was genuinely evil as she impersonated the sound of a gun. "POW!"

Then Gina turned to cameraman Jesse as she continued steering the car. The expression on her face had completely changed.

"Get your hand out of the window before you fall out the car. Why you aggravatin' me?" She sounded like a bossy mom scolding her child.

Jesse replied meekly: "I ain't aggravatin' you."

Gina snapped back, "Now you're really aggravatin' me."

Gina's sister Jody remains angry to this day that Jesse Dunn did not report her sister's wish to kill her husband to the police.

She recalled: "I was kinda mad at him because I felt he could have said something to stop it."

In reality Jesse was so alarmed by Gina's outbursts that one day at the house on Old Waynesboro Road he tried to warn Kevin Spann. Spann was disturbed by what he heard but chose to take little notice of it.

Jesse even expressed deep regret and sorrow for the trouble he'd caused by moving into the house. He reiterated his warning to Kevin that he should get out of the house because he was convinced that Gina was going to try and have him killed.

Kevin Spann felt no one had the right to remove him from his own home. He even suspected that Jesse might be lying just because he wanted the house to himself and Gina.

TWELVE

One of the younger members of the staff at Taco Bell who watched Gina Spann turn from a housewife into a drug-obsessed party girl was Amanda Quick.

She and Gina earned $4.75 an hour at the restaurant. Both worked stints as cashiers at the drive-thru window. "It got real busy at lunch and supper time," recalled Amanda. They also regularly changed jobs within the restaurant as part of the company policy to avoid on-the-job boredom.

Amanda Quick found Gina awkward to communicate with. "She didn't seem to like talkin' to girls. I noticed she changed whenever a guy was nearby. She reacted better to them, I guess."

Amanda also happened to be a young, attractive blonde with a stream of boys and men taking an interest in virtually her every move.

She quickly became wary of Gina. Amanda couldn't understand why Gina's husband never dropped by to see her in the restaurant. "I tried to get her to talk about him but she kept changin' the subject although she did mention her son."

At first Amanda Quick had no idea that a teenager was living at Gina's house, having a relationship with her. "I was kinda surprised when I later found out about that. I never had any idea. She kept it real quiet from the rest of the women at Taco Bell. Reckon she knew what we'd all say."

Then Gina got Jesse a job as a cleaner at Taco Bell. She had insisted Jesse work because she could ill afford to support her own drink and drug habits, let alone his.

But by the time Jesse got the job, Gina had already begun spending more and more time with other boys who worked in the restaurant, as well as some youths who were regular customers. Amanda Quick and many of the other Taco Bell staff were appalled by her behavior.

"We reckoned she was some kinda creep. She just wouldn't stay away from the young boys. It was real weird," Amanda said.

Towards the fall of 1996 Gina's friends and family noticed that she was getting increasingly unhappy about her life. She'd snap at anyone who dared to disagree with her and she was very pessimistic about the future.

Holding down a job, taking a lot of drugs, servicing a young lover and living in the same house as her estranged husband and young son was taking a heavy toll. She was also worried that Kevin would take up a new posting out of the area, which could bring forward any divorce plans.

Gina threw herself into an even more intense round of drinking and drug-taking in an effort to drown her depression. That meant she stayed out of the house on Old Waynesboro virtually every night.

On one of the rare days when Gina and Kevin Spann were in the house at the same time they had a confrontation about what to do with their marriage. Kevin suggested immediate divorce. It was hardly a surprise.

But Gina was upset by Kevin's attitude. She wanted to be the one to decide when it was time to get divorced. Kevin had always been quiet and reserved and she'd always been the boss and that was the way she intended to keep it.

In any case, Gina had another, far more greedy motive. She knew she would get a very small divorce settlement and no part of Kevin's relatively lucrative Army pension and saving plan. Gina was facing virtual poverty as a single mom while he could walk away, start a new life, marry and have children of his own and probably even afford to actually buy a house. Gina didn't like even thinking about it.

So she ignored Kevin's request for a divorce and played for time by keeping out of his way while she worked out how to keep that money.

If Kevin Spann had been a stronger person he might have nailed Gina down at that moment. But he never pursued her vigorously enough and her stalling tactics worked effectively over the next few months. She had already informed Kevin that she and Jesse had nowhere to live and would have to stay at the house at least until the current lease expired in the summer of 1997.

So, despite Kevin's talk of divorce, Gina continued staying out all hours taking drugs and boozing at local bars. And not always in the company of young Jesse, who was becoming increasingly unhappy about the living arrangements.

When Jason Swallow told Gina that he was having problems with his family at home she encouraged him to move into the house for a rent of $100 a month. Not only would it help ease her financial problems but it was also another diversion for Kevin to deal with. Within days Jason had moved his water bed into the den of the house.

It quickly became obvious to Jason that there were big problems between Gina and Kevin. "But, you know, I never heard Gina actually fighting with Kevin. Never."

While Jason lived in the house on Old Waynesboro Road, a bizarre ritual was established which was intended to avoid awkward confrontations. "I noticed they made a real point never to come 'cross each other inside the house."

Jason explained: "If Kevin was in the kitchen then Gina would stay in the sitting room and vice versa. Kevin even had a little corner of the icebox where he kept his food and drink and we were told by Gina never to touch that stuff. I got used to it after a while and it seemed to work okay."

Back at Taco Bell, Gina was getting increasingly short-tempered with both customers and staff. "She'd lose her cool real easy with difficult customers. But then she most often had a real bad hangover 'cause she was taking a lot of drugs at the time," added Jason.

Gina told some of her young friends and colleagues that she was fed up with not being promoted by Taco Bell. She told them she needed to earn more money in order to pay for the cost of her home and her son. In fact most of her money was going to booze and dope.

She got even more fed up when a younger member of the Taco Bell staff was made assistant manager.

Around this time Gina Spann began working alongside a 19-year-old named Michael Kelley on the food counter. Some of the other staff immediately presumed they were having some kind of a relationship because Gina got into the habit of squeezing Michael's arm playfully and giggling in his direction.

Her behavior upset many of Gina's new young friends at Taco Bell. "Jesse didn't deserve to have her cheatin' on him. And he was even working out back in the kitchens at the time. I reckoned he'd find out soon enough," explained Jason Swallow.

But Gina was actually only flirting with Michael Kelley, who has always insisted he had absolutely no interest in her.

Then Kelley's 17-year-old brother Larry joined the staff of Taco Bell. Larry was six feet tall, weighed a trim 150 pounds and had dark wavy hair and steely gray-blue eyes. Every teenage girl he encountered in the restaurant was most impressed.

As Amanda Quick admitted: "You couldn't help noticing Larry. He was a good-looking guy in a dark Italian kinda way."

Larry Kelley was very much living in the shadow of his older brother Michael. He'd been one of the less noticeable students at nearby Butler High.

"He was a bit indecisive, I guess. You weren't always too sure if there was a lot goin' on inside his head if you get what I mean," added Amanda.

Larry Kelley's family did not live in a trailer park, but in a very modest neighborhood of south Richmond County. However, inside that house were nearly thirty dogs in cages. Sometimes the children must have wondered if their mother loved her animals more than her kids.

Shy Larry Kelley hardly talked to anyone in those early days at Taco Bell.

Gina thought he was extremely handsome. There was something about his dark, sullen eyes that she found most enticing. But any notion of her starting a romance with Kelley seemed ludicrous. Gina was thirty years old, weighed well over 200 pounds by this stage and had returned to her jeans-and-sneakers style which made her look like just about every overweight housewife in Augusta.

Back at Taco Bell there were soon rumors flying around that handsome Larry Kelley was dating one of the female employees.

Revealed Jason Swallow: "No one was surprised he was dating someone but we all got a hell of shock when we found out it was Gina. Hey, it wasn't none of my business but I didn't like to see Jesse hurt. He was a cool guy and he'd done nothing to deserve bein' cheated on."

At first Gina simply seemed to be flirting with Larry, just as she had with his brother Michael. Then Jesse began working different shifts from Gina.

"She'd head off someplace from Taco Bell at the end of a shift. I heard that she and Larry would go to a motel," explained Jason. "At first she kept it all secret from Jesse 'cause I was going back to her house on Waynesboro every night and there was no way Jesse had any idea what was goin' down."

Many of Gina's young friends noticed that Gina's dark moods were easing off. And her so-called secret affair was becoming fodder for the Taco Bell gossips.

However, Jason Swallow became convinced that Gina was planning something more than just an illicit romance.

"I got the feelin' she was up to something. It was like she'd always be whispering to Larry and then looking real serious. Like she was the teacher and he was her pupil. Does that make sense?"

Jason and some of the others at Taco Bell began wondering if there was some hidden agenda behind Gina's continual chasing of young guys. "She wanted something from them and it sure as hell wasn't their minds," added Jason.

A short time after this, Jason Swallow found out what was really going on . . .

THIRTEEN

One quiet morning Gina was working alongside Jason at Taco Bell when she made a strange request completely out of the blue.

"Can I borrow your gun, Jason?"

Jason couldn't quite believe his ears.

"What?"

"Can you loan me that gun you bought?"

"How d'you know 'bout that?"

"Everyone in here knows."

Gina paused for a split second, then softened the tone of her voice.

"Please?"

Jason was perturbed to be asked such a question. It seemed that everyone at Taco Bell knew he'd just bought the black .25 semi-automatic from another Taco Bell employee.

"But I didn't like the way she asked," he later recalled. "She said she just needed it for a night. She tried to make it sound like it was real normal."

"Why d'you want it?" asked Jason at the time.

"For a reason . . ."

"What reason?"

"That's my business."

"If you don't tell me, then how the hell can I loan it you?"

Jason later recalled: "I didn't know what she wanted that gun for but I had a feelin' it was something bad. That's why I didn't loan it [to] her. I also wondered whether it was time to quit that house on Waynesboro Road."

A few days later Taco Bell co-worker Joe Harrod heard about Gina's attempt to borrow a gun from Jason Swallow.

"Don't give her it. She's got some crazy scheme to kill her husband," Harrod told him.

"What?" replied a surprised Jason Swallow.

"Just don't give her the fucking gun, man."

Back on the romantic front it had became extremely clear to many at Taco Bell that Gina and Larry Kelley were serious about each other. The staff were increasingly unsettled by the sight of them kissing and cuddling at the counter.

Jason Swallow noted: "It was so blatant, you know what I mean? They'd be giggling, tickling each other. A lot of folk just didn't approve. They were being too fuckin' open 'bout it."

One older lady employee at Taco Bell told Jason Swallow: "Who the hell does that Gina Spann think she is? That kid's nearly young enough to be her son."

Larry Kelley was in fact a 17-year-old virgin completely overwhelmed by Gina's attentions. As one of his friends later explained: "Larry was desperate to lose it and he believed that someone like Gina would teach him a thing or two."

Jesse Dunn believed that their relationship was falling apart because he'd refused to respond to her request to kill her husband rather than let him divorce her.

Jesse never had the courage to confront Gina about her affair with Kelley, despite what many of his friends were telling him about the youth he had already nicknamed "Crazy Larry."

He explained: "I knew there was somethin' goin' on but that Larry guy was crazy. He scared the shit outta me. Reckon they were capable of anything."

Gina seemed oblivious to the rumors and continued to date Larry by going out with him right after work, leaving Jesse to make his own way back to the house.

Then Jesse did her a favor and quit his job.

He explained: "I couldn't stand it no more so I, I quit. There was a bunch of stuff going on. She was pissing me off and I couldn't stand to be around it and . . . I had a suspicion, but I didn't know for sure."

Yet, bizarrely, Jesse continued to live at the house with Michael and Kevin. He had nowhere else to go. "They treated me real good. Think they felt kinda sorry for me in some ways. Guess they knew how much trouble Gina could be."

Jesse also began thinking more and more about some of the things Gina had been saying to him about killing her husband.

"While I was with her she had joked about doing things to Kevin. Just, off-the-wall jokes about insurance money and stuff like that and, you know, I'm thinking, you know, she was just talking, you know.

I mean, she used the term 'kill,' 'get rid of' and stuff like that all the time."

One day she even suggested to Jesse they should get Kevin drunk and drown him.

"You're crazy," Jesse told her before yet again changing the subject.

Jesse later recalled, "She even talked about insurance. I think she said something like, she said it was like five hundred thousand dollars or something like that."

In November 1996 Gina even let slip to Jesse that she'd spoken to Larry about blowing up Kevin Spann's car.

"Apparently they were planning on putting something in his car and blowing it up with him in it or something," said Jesse.

Meanwhile Jesse's lack of work and Gina's continuing affair with Larry was driving an inevitable wedge between them.

Gina stayed out at night and Jesse ended up being unofficial babysitter most of the time. He was also well aware that Gina was taking a lot of drugs.

But Jesse's main concern at the time was Gina's son.

He later explained: "Michael was a very troubled child. I really felt for him. He was a nice kid but he never really had a mother in the normal sense.

"Maybe Gina did mean well towards him but he always seemed to be left out of things. I noticed he had behavioral problems. He like acted out a lot and had temper tantrums and you can't tell me that wasn't due to his life at the time.

"I mean, she'd come home at all hours of the night and I'd tell her, you know, 'I wish you'd stay home and come home from work,' and, but she was out running around with the, the whole young teenager crew."

Jesse believes to this day that there were other men in Gina's life, as well.

"Of course there were other guys. There was, shoot, I don't want to get anybody like involved that really doesn't want to be."

Jesse was never quite sure about the relationship between Gina and roommate Jason Swallow, although Jason later insisted there was nothing between them.

Throughout this period, Jesse continued keeping the house clean and watching young Michael.

One strange side-effect of all this was that Jesse's relationship with Kevin Spann continued to improve.

He explained: "Kevin would be in the kitchen and I'd be in the kitchen and Kevin and I actually had conversations about the way Gina was."

They got to talking about their frustrations over Gina's behavior.

Jesse even asked him: "Have you ever known her to lie?"

"All the time," came the reply.

"Watch out," Jesse told him. "She's capable of anything."

"Yeah. I've known that for years," came Kevin's deadpan response.

As Jesse later pointed out: "It was all kinda weird because Kevin knew I'd been intimate with her."

And to this day Jesse refuses to believe that Kevin ever abused Gina.

"Like I say, I never, ever . . . I never even seen the man raise a hand. Not even being loud and boisterous or fussin', cursin' or any damn thing. Never."

Jesse also never forgot how Kevin Spann always maintained a calm voice even when he was talking to his wife in the house.

He added: "That's the reason I talked to him in the first place. I mean, if you were in my situation would you even talk to the husband on the other end of the house?"

Meanwhile Jesse continued to have problems with Larry Kelley and his brother Michael.

"I heard later that Michael was real upset that his little brother got involved with such a crazy person or something like that."

Larry Kelley had been living in various friends' homes since June 1996 when he left home because of problems he was having with his stepfather. Both Larry and Michael later claimed that that was one of the main reasons they both ended up dropping out of Butler High School.

Michael explained: "It's hard to try to work and live on your own and go to school. It gets frustrating. At the school they just gave up on us after we got into a little trouble. But we were beginning to get on the right track and finish school."

That's when Larry and Gina started their relationship.

"I guess Larry thought he was in love with her. I think the fact she was an older woman. And she could give him stuff he couldn't get, like drugs, and she was sleeping with him."

Michael then repeated what a number of Gina's younger friends felt was true: "Gina Spann had become a mother figure to many of the teenagers who worked in Taco Bell. Those with problems felt like they could talk to her and she wouldn't judge them. When you first met her she seemed, like, real cool."

He laid blame for both his own and his brother's drug use squarely at the feet of Gina Spann.

"Me and Larry never used any drugs until we met up with her. She gave Larry and the other boys acid, alcohol and marijuana.

"She was always inviting me to her house. She said she and her husband had an open marriage, and that if I was there and he woke up in the morning, he would just step over me and everybody else—that was all there was to it."

Michael claimed that in January 1997 he himself had been asked by Gina to kill her husband.

"I got this plan to get my husband out of the way. You gonna help me?" she asked him as they sat in the front room at the house on Old Waynesboro Road.

"No way. I'm tryin' to keep outta trouble," replied Michael Kelley.

"No one'll know," said Gina.

"Look, Gina, I been in jail once before and I never want to go back."

Meanwhile Jesse Dunn had other more practical problems to consider, particularly that he had no place to move, so he couldn't leave the house. It was a catch-22 for the jobless youth, so he decided to try and ignore what was happening virtually in front of his eyes.

Roommate Jason Swallow saw Gina's increasingly tangled love life as a signal for him to finally move out.

"I knew it was time to leave. The atmosphere inside the house went real bad after Gina started dating Larry because it became clear she wanted Jesse out of the house."

Jason was much more concerned about Gina's deteriorating relationship with Jesse than her weird marriage to Kevin. He and his friends continued to disapprove of the way in which she'd dumped Jesse for Larry.

At work, the management got so fed up with Gina's behavior that they insisted she transfer to another Taco Bell near the center of Augusta. It was another sign for Jason Swallow to leave the house; Gina would no longer be able to give him a ride into Taco Bell because she was going to work at a branch on 19th Street. "That swung it for me. I had to get outta there quickly," Jason recounted.

Throughout this period Gina pressured Jesse at every available opportunity to leave the house so she could move Larry in. While she never actually stated that that was her intention, she did admit she'd fallen in love with Larry and that had a profound effect on Jesse Dunn.

He later recalled: "I realize now that she was just a born liar. She just didn't know how to tell the truth. She hurt me so bad. I don't know what I saw in her. She just used me."

And Jason Swallow was just as perplexed. "I didn't get it; how could she just fall in and out of love so easy? What did she want out of these relationships?"

Back at the house, Jesse became increasingly isolated by the events happening around him.

Jason explained: "Jesse wasn't from around these parts so he didn't have no friends or nothin' and he had no place to go. For a few weeks he stayed in the house and the atmosphere got real bad."

The other person stuck in the middle of this extremely unhealthy love triangle was 12-year-old Michael. He became increasingly withdrawn and hardly spoke to anyone except Kevin, who was creeping in in the dead of night and rising so early in the morning that he was rarely seen.

To confuse matters, Gina continued sharing a bed with Jesse while he remained in the house. It was almost as if she had to have someone in her bed even though she intended to replace him with another man.

Then one day Jesse bought himself a plane ticket and headed back to Virginia. No one at the house on Old Waynesboro ever saw or heard from him again. Recalled Jason: "It was a real shame 'cause he was a cool guy. I tried to get Gina to give me his e-mail address but she refused. Think she was scared he might tell me a few home truths about her."

Hours after Jesse's departure, Gina moved Larry Kelley into the house. She couldn't bear to be alone in bed, even for one night.

FOURTEEN

Another Taco Bell employee who found himself embroiled in Gina's tangled love life was 21-year-old Joe Harrod. He started hanging out with Gina after she fell for Larry Kelley, who happened to be Harrod's roommate at the time.

Gina spent many hours at Harrod's house with Larry talking about her frustrations with life.

"I got to know them real good," recalled Harrod. "At first I thought Kevin was a real nice man and Gina, well, she was nice, too."

But soon after Gina began her friendship with Harrod and his wife she began telling him that her husband had raped and attacked her. She also moaned to Harrod that her then live-in boyfriend Jesse refused to do anything about it. She even suggested that Harrod and Larry Kelley could kill Kevin and easily make it look as if someone had broken into the house.

"Gina was giving us all these sob stories about Kevin beating her up, so that obviously made Larry mad and he talked several times about if he [Kevin] did it again he'd kill him," recalled Joe.

Shortly after this Joe had to throw Larry out of his home because the teenager had incurred huge phone bills by making calls to sex lines. It was then that Larry moved into Gina's home.

Larry Kelley's own recollections of his affair with Gina include a claim that she persuaded him to move into her house by assuring him that she had an open marriage.

The age difference between them was perfectly summed up when Larry explained: "So I packed up my clothes, my comic books, video games and my toy dinosaur collection and headed over to that house."

It wasn't long before Gina started telling her young lover about plans to supposedly divorce her allegedly brutal husband.

As one of Gina's oldest friends pointed out: "I called 'round the day Larry moved in and there they were together in bed. Gina didn't like sleepin' alone, that was for sure. She didn't even bother to tell her husband or son what was happening. She didn't seem to care."

As Gina's sexual appetite needed satisfying, so did her need for drugs—weed, acid, crack, even speed. She couldn't get enough of it. That meant a lot of other kids continued hanging out at the house looking for a piece of the action.

Gina tried to be careful to make sure her son Mike wasn't awake when the drugs were used. But that didn't stop them from being consumed on the premises the moment she thought Mike was asleep. Many of Gina's friends remain convinced to this day that the child must have known what was happening.

*　　*　　*

Then,. after weeks of self-torture and non-communication with his wife, Kevin Spann finally put his foot down following a particularly rowdy evening during which he hardly got any sleep.

One friend explained: "Kevin went ballistic at Gina after everyone had split. Even she realized she'd pushed it too far."

Gina was worried that he would go ahead with the divorce proceedings and possibly even call the police.

But once again she ignored the divorce issue and decided to rent a room over at one of the seedy flop-houses on the Peach Orchard strip whenever she wanted to party. She somehow managed to pacify Kevin, who left the house that morning no nearer to sorting out his crumbling marriage.

Many of Gina's young friends reckoned that one of the main reasons Gina kicked Jesse was out because he'd stopped being her virtual slave. Gina liked to bark orders at him and at first he'd done exactly what he was told. "It was like he was some kind of pet pooch. But then he wouldn't do what she said and that's when Gina turned to Larry. He was like putty in her hands."

Gina herself told one friend that she loved Larry Kelley because: "Most of the time he doesn't say much of anything but he just holds me and smiles. Then when I shout at him he gets that sad look on his face and tells me he's sorry."

She needed complete and utter subservience from the men in her life.

Not long after Larry Kelley moved into the house, Kevin Spann shook Gina by announcing that he would soon be transferred to Fort Knox. Gina feared that could mean he'd step up the pressure for a divorce. One friend called in at the house and heard Gina trying to turn the whole issue into a joke. "She was kiddin' around with Larry about ways to break in and steal some gold from Fort Knox. I thought they were high at the time but now I'm not so sure. But I knew from the way that Gina was speaking that she was real pissed about it."

That was when Gina told Larry, his brother Michael and their friends that Kevin had started hitting her again.

Gina told Michael and Larry for at least the third time that she was afraid of divorcing Kevin because she'd lose her treasured Cavalier convertible. Then she lowered her voice and looked at Michael.

"Help me kill Kevin. You'd make Larry so happy if you did that . . ."

Michael ignored Gina's request just as he had the first time she'd asked him to murder her husband.

What he didn't realize was that Gina had already begun exerting pressure on Larry by suggesting that she might be pregnant with his baby.

She told Larry that she wasn't certain yet. But Gina wanted to make him truly belong to her.

Not long after this, ex-roommate Jason Swallow dropped by the house to pick up some clothes he'd left behind when he moved back home. He recalled: "The atmosphere was really weird. Place reeked of weed. When I walked in both Gina and Larry went real quiet, as if they'd been discussing something private. I only got to thinking about it afterwards."

Others who visited the house said that the atmosphere changed drastically after Gina took Larry Kelley into her bed. There was a sinister undercurrent in the air. Something was being planned but no one knew what.

Soon after that Jason Swallow quit his job at Taco Bell and got himself a better-paying job as a dishwasher at Giuseppes Restaurant on Peach Orchard.

He never talked to Gina or Larry again. "Guess I was one of the lucky ones," he later surmised.

Meanwhile Gina was piling the pressure on Larry Kelley to help her kill "brutal wife-beater" Kevin Spann. She also became far more specific about how she intended to do it. One of Gina's early suggestions was to choke Kevin and throw him in a lake. The second plan was just to shoot him.

To a kid like Larry Kelley it all sounded like something out of a movie. The only time he'd ever been in trouble with the law was when he was stopped in the street by police and gave them a false name and address because he was afraid his stepfather might get angry with him.

Larry's understanding of reality had been blurred by an emotional void created partly through bland video games, horror movies and a complete lack of conscience. As Gina talked he just nodded and agreed without ever once thinking about the consequences of what she was saying.

In January 1997, Kevin Spann became so distraught about the state of his loveless, sexless marriage that he traveled up to his hometown of Lebanon, Illinois, to ask his father for advice on what to do.

While in the area he also dropped in at Gina's mom Sue's house to see what she and Gina's sister Jody Pierce reckoned he should do to sort out the situation.

Jody was typically blunt: "It's time you heard some home truths, Kevin," she told her brother-in-law. "Gina's been scamming you for so long and you don't seem to have worked it out. You gotta get away from her. Forget her before she bleeds you dry."

Kevin Spann looked deeply upset by what Jody said. He admitted he'd come up to Illinois to get away from Gina and the man she was sleeping with but now he was being made to face up to reality—and it hurt.

Jody continued: "Just pack your stuff and get outta that house 'cause otherwise you'll end up losin' your temper and takin' out one of those kids she's been sleepin' with.

"Then you're gonna get in real trouble, Kevin."

Kevin nodded his head in agreement and remembered another aspect of the situation that had been bothering him for a long time.

"I got this insurance policy that's worth a lot of money. If I get divorced she'll lose it and she knows it. Problem is I can't even afford to pay off the remainder of the lease on the house 'til I get this tax rebate I'm expectin'."

Jody later recalled: "He was completely under her sleeve. If he kicked her out he wouldn't get the money from the military to support the family and he wouldn't be able to live without it. Gina knew that and that was why she was sticking around until someone richer came along."

Ironically both Gina and Kevin believed that they could not economically afford to live apart, despite the appalling state of their marriage. It was a no-win situation and each was waiting for the other to make a move.

Back in Augusta just a few weeks later, Kevin, for some bizarre reason, decided to try yet again to save his marriage, despite the presence of Larry Kelley in the house.

None of his friends or relatives could understand why he would bother but he felt it was worth one last chance. "He reckoned that if he co-operated with her then she might kick Larry Kelley out of her bed and they could go back to the way things had been," explained old friend Nathan Blake.

As part of that final attempt to win her back, Kevin even bought Gina the swimming pool he'd been promising her ever since they'd moved into the house. It was an above-ground pool but it still set the hard-pressed serviceman back $4,000 on a high interest repayment deal over 36 months.

Kevin set up the pool in the back yard and had it waiting for Gina when she got home from Taco Bell one day. Gina took it as a peace gesture and later told her new young friends that Kevin was obviously try-ing to buy her co-operation to avoid any police action over the beatings he'd inflicted on her. She'd told so many people about Kevin's "brutality" by this time, that she'd started to believe her own web of lies.

By trying to buy his way back into Gina's affections, Kevin Spann was running up even more debts, mak-ing it virtually impossible for him to ease off the exhausting work schedule he was committed to. When Kevin tried to confront Gina about the situation she simply walked away.

"Kevin had so many expenses with Gina that he had no choice but keep working those three jobs. I used to say it would be the death of him," recalled Jody.

But Kevin's generosity did not have the desired effect on his marriage. Gina made no attempt to move Larry Kelley out of the house.

When it finally dawned on Kevin that he wasn't going to save his marriage he switched to a harder tactic that almost blew up badly in his face.

"He told Gina he was definitely going to seek a divorce and that made her real mad because she knew she'd lose the support money from the army for Michael," recalled Jody.

So Gina came up with a thinly veiled threat. "If you make me leave the house I'll call the Army and tell them that Mike wasn't living here in the first place," she bitterly told Kevin. "Then you'll get in trouble and lose the extra money. Don't reckon you'll be able to pay the bills then, d'you?"

As sister Jody later explained: "She was blackmailing him. She was sticking it to him no matter what."

In February 1997, Kevin Spann received two threatening letters accusing him of beating up Gina and warning him to leave the house immediately or face the consequences.

Kevin was extremely worried by these letters but he didn't go to the police about them. Instead he mentioned the threats when he met up with fellow soldier Donald Leroy Keller Jr., who was based with Kevin at Fort Gordon.

Keller never actually saw the threatening notes but Kevin was convinced they were from his wife's boyfriend. Kevin also told Keller that his wife Gina was addicted to the Internet.

"She's on it day and night," he said, without specifically mentioning that she had met her previous young lover that way.

Kevin Spann made it clear to his friend that he was distraught about his wife's behavior but he didn't know how to deal with it.

Kevin had been friends with Keller for some years and had mentioned his marital problems to him in the past. But this time he told Keller that his wife's boyfriend lived in the same house. Keller was appalled.

He didn't know how to advise his friend except to say that he should remain calm because there was no way anyone would do anything to harm him.

Kevin Spann in an official U.S. Army photo taken twelve months before his murder.

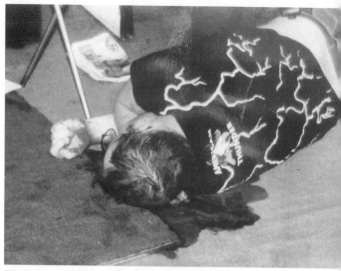

The body of Kevin Spann, photographed less than an hour after he was killed. (Augusta Police Department)

The front entrance to the Spann house. Kevin Spann's legs can be seen in the open doorway. (Augusta Police Department)

An aerial view of the house on Old Waynesboro and the surrounding woods and fields where the two youths ran following the killing. The Spann house is in the center of the photo. (Augusta Police Department)

The white Toyota that Horne and Piazzi stole after their failed attempt to kill Kevin Spann. (Augusta Police Department)

Jason Swallow lived at the Spann house and worked with Gina at Taco Bell.
(Wensley Clarkson)

Amanda Quick had a strange encounter with the killers of Kevin Spann just before they carried out the murder.
(Wensley Clarkson)

Gina Spann in the video that she made with teenage lover Jesse Dunn during which she openly discussed killing her husband. (Augusta District Attorney's Office)

Larry Kelley's defense attorney, Mike Garrett, believes to this day that Kelley should not have been convicted of murder. (Wensley Clarkson)

Augusta DA Danny Craig and his prose-cuting team member Nancy Johnson.
(Wensley Clarkson)

Augusta Police investigator Jimmy Vowell.
(Wensley Clarkson)

The Taco Bell on Peach Orchard Road where Gina Spann worked and met teenage lovers. (Wensley Clarkson)

The car trunk where Gina hid insurance documents before she tried getting her sister to hide them from police investigators. (Augusta Police Department)

The Royal Palms Motel on Peach Orchard where the killers lived the week before the killing. (Wensley Clarkson)

Matt Piazzi

Police mug shots taken the morning after Kevin Spann's murder.
(Augusta Police Department)

Gina Spann

Gerry Horne

FIFTEEN

In the middle of April 1997, Kevin called Jody in Belleville and told her he was close to the breaking point. "I'm just waiting for my income tax rebate and then I'll pay off the lease and get the hell outta here," Kevin told her. "I'm outta here. Period."

But Jody knew her sister only too well.

"It won't be that easy, Kevin," she replied. "Gina sees it as her job to keep you and all your money. Simple as that."

Then Kevin brought up the subject of the various insurance policies. It was a conversation that Jody has never forgotten to this day.

She recalled: "He started talking about the insurance policies again and if anything ever happened to him, Mike would have college money available."

Then Kevin Spann told his sister-in-law: "The only reason I stuck it out as long as I have is because of Michael. I want to make sure that Michael is taken care of."

Jody later recalled: "All the stuff that was going around him was scaring him that Mike wouldn't be okay. He wanted that boy to have a good life whatever shit was going down around him."

But Jody knew that the situation would not be resolved as easily as Kevin seemed to think.

"You see, Gina pretty much got whatever she wanted. She didn't have to work for anything. Growing up she learned how to manipulate men and knowing how not to work got her into a lot of trouble. I knew she was scared that the money was going to go and no one would be there to take care of her.

"Me and my mom knew she was headin' down the wrong road. We didn't know how she'd deal with it. But we knew she'd just get into more and more trouble and my main concern was getting Kevin out of the middle of it."

In early April 1997, Gina Spann returned to work at Taco Bell on the Peach Orchard strip after the 19th Street Augusta branch closed down.

Some time after Larry Kelley had moved into the house on Old Waynesboro Road, Michael Kelley made a biting comment to Amanda Quick about the relationship between his kid brother and Gina.

"My mom and dad are real pissed about Larry goin' with Gina," said Michael. "It's gonna end in trouble."

Amanda wasn't surprised. She later explained: "Some of us girls at Taco Bell still had a bad kinda feeling 'bout Gina. She was trouble. We couldn't work her out.

"They were like the stars of their very own daytime soap. Every morning we'd all get an update on the latest about Larry and Gina.

"They'd be foolin' around whenever the staff and customers weren't looking. There was even this other guy called Jim who also hung out at the Taco Bell a lot. He seemed to know them well. I never worked out how the hell he knew so much. Some of us thought he might be sleeping with Gina as well."

Then in the middle of April 1997 Kevin visited his friend Donald Keller at his home inside Fort Gordon. The following Monday Spann was due to go for a week to a training camp at Fort Jackson in South Carolina.

The two men went out and shot some pool and talked about old times. Then Kevin took Keller back to the house he still shared with Gina. But when the two men arrived in Kevin's car, he turned the car engine off and just sat there without moving. "I thought that was strange," Keller said later, "and so I asked him if something was wrong."

Kevin Spann's reply surprised his friend: "I'm afraid of goin' home. I'm worried about her friends and the crowd she's hangin' with. They're drug-users and living off us to support their habit. They're capable of anything to get more money."

Keller was doubly shocked because the Kevin Spann he had known at Fort Gordon was a strong, courageous soldier and yet here he was nervous about stepping inside his own home.

But Kevin Spann refused to go to the police. He still believed he could sort it all out himself.

Some time after the dispute about telephone bills, Joe Harrod started seeing Gina and Larry once again. They had a bizarre conversation when Joe was driving them in his van after they'd picked up some takeout pizzas.

"You gonna help me kill Kevin for his insurance money?" Gina Spann asked Harrod.

Harrod said nothing at first.

Then Larry chipped in: "Let's do it tonight. It'll be easy, man."

Joe Harrod could feel the pressure they were trying to put him under. Then his wife Ashley Michelle spoke up.

"No way."

Harrod himself reiterated by saying: "It's no. That's it."

As Harrod turned his van into the trailer park where he lived he made a point of saying it again.

Gina persisted.

Harrod started to lose his cool. "That's nothing to even talk about, Gina. Just drop it."

But Gina wouldn't drop it. "There's this big insurance policy he's got. I'll give you half the money if you help me kill him."

A few seconds elapsed before she continued. "So, you gonna help me kill my husband or what?"

Harrod was shocked. "I told you, you don't even need to be saying that kinda stuff."

Harrod sensed that Gina was enjoying the subject—and she would not let go that easily. She started laying the details of how she wanted her husband shot. She even told her three friends: "We can bury him out here and no one will ever find him."

Gina also made it perfectly clear that she could lay her hands on a gun without much trouble—by stealing it from Larry's stepfather. "All we have to do is go in and make it look like the house had been burglarized."

Harrod later claimed that the evening ended in tension with Gina and Larry departing from the Harrod trailer in a huff.

Not long after that—in the third week of April 1997—Gina dropped in at Harrod's house to talk to Ashley Michelle while he was at work.

Harrod interpreted that visit as a sign that they could all be friends again and all four went out and had a pizza together a few days later.

That night they all went back to the house on Old Waynesboro. Kevin Spann showed up halfway through the evening with Gina's son Mike.

The moment Kevin arrived the atmosphere, not surprisingly, changed drastically.

Michael walked into the front room and told Gina that Kevin wanted to speak to her. Gina disappeared into the kitchen. Moments later Harrod heard them arguing and fighting. Then the back door slammed and they heard Kevin's car driving off at high speed.

Gina tried to convince her friends that Kevin's behavior that night was further evidence of how cruel he was being to her. She made a point of telling Larry in front of the Harrods how bad things with Kevin were.

Not long after this, Gina and Larry turned up at Joe Harrod's home and she once again brought up the subject.

Right in the middle of dinner she looked up and said: "I'm gonna kill Kevin one day."

Harrod looked at Gina. He couldn't believe she was saying it yet again. "Why would you want to kill him?"

"He's got money."

"Gina, you know, if you kill him you're not going to get away with it. You don't need to do that."

But Gina wouldn't be that easily deterred.

"Come on. Why don't you get in on it? I'll split the money with you."

"Gina, we don't want no part of it, none whatsoever because we don't want to get in no trouble. We do not want to kill anybody whatsoever. Any case I like Kevin."

As Harrod later explained: "I'd met him several times and I mean, you know, he was nice to me and you know, I liked him."

But then Gina backtracked: "Well, you know I'm not really gonna do this. I'm just joking around."

Harrod was willing to take her at her word: He'd heard it all before and he didn't think she was serious about her plans to murder her husband.

But he did notice that Gina made it perfectly clear to her friends that she had asked Larry to kill her husband. In fact she had continued to tell Larry that her husband was raping her and beating her. She was convinced that eventually he'd do something about it.

And then there was the pregnancy. By this time Gina had told Larry categorically that she was expecting his baby. It had the desired effect of making the impressionable, emotionally stunted teenager believe that he was involved in a relationship for life, which meant protecting the woman he loved—and their baby—from her brutal, uncaring husband.

When Kevin Spann began his training course at Fort Jackson in Columbia, South Carolina, it meant he was even more exhausted on the rare nights when he did manage the long drive home. And he still had the other two part-time jobs to hold down.

Despite the breakdown of their marriage, Gina still felt insecure about whether he had another girlfriend. Gina was looking for excuses to hurt Kevin and his trips away from home were perfect fodder for her twisted mind.

Gina and Larry had psychologically committed to each other that they would kill Kevin Spann. It was just a matter of how and when.

In the early hours of Saturday morning on April 18, 1997, intruders broke into the home of Larry Kelley's stepfather David Best on Margaret Court, in Hephzibah. The burglars broke a pane of glass in the back door before reaching in and unlocking it. Then they crept into the master bedroom and ransacked it.

Best later told police that fifty dollars in quarters, a diamond dinner ring, a gold wedding band and two Minolta cameras had been stolen. He did not inform police that a .38 gun he owned was also missing. Whether this was because he genuinely did not know or because it was an unregistered weapon will never be known. He also informed investigating officer Greg Newsome that he suspected his own stepsons Larry and Michael of carrying out the crime, because they were the only people who would have known where the money was hidden.

Actually Larry had carried out the burglary while Gina sat outside waiting in her car. They were now partners in crime.

Larry Kelley continued to believe that his lover's husband was a wife-beater and he saw it as his duty to help her get rid of him. However, Larry was not keen on carrying out the killing himself. For a few weeks he tried to bluff his way through by assuring Gina that he would do it when the time was right. But Gina soon realized that Larry did not have the courage to carry it out himself. He would have to look further afield to achieve his lover's ultimate goal.

Gina suggested that Larry should try and find someone outside his circle of immediate friends to carry out the hit on Kevin so that they could distance themselves from the crime.

Larry looked up an acquaintance named Chris Bargeron who'd met Gina before when he'd been hanging out at the Taco Bell.

Bargeron hardly exuded the sort of confidence one would expect from a would-be hitman. He was a bloated-looking greasy-haired 16-year-old weighing in at almost 250 pounds.

But despite his appearance, Bargeron was actually a very wise head on old shoulders. He assured Kelley that he would take care of their "problem" but told Kelley it would cost $15,000.

Gina reckoned that was a small price to pay in order to get rid of Kevin—especially since she knew his life insurance policies would pay out $300,000 in the event of his death.

Chris Bargeron was completely undeterred by the fact that he had been asked to be a hitman at the age of 16. His response was so calm, Larry Kelley worried that maybe the youth had smoked too much weed that day.

Bargeron immediately took control of the operation. He laid out the plan in careful detail to Larry and Gina and they presumed that their murderous scheme was now in safe hands.

Kelley and Gina believed that Bargeron would be the triggerman. Bargeron did nothing to contradict this until it got closer to the time when the crime was supposed to be committed.

What they didn't realize was that he had already started asking around Butler High School whether any of the kids knew someone greedy and crazy enough "to kill a guy for some big bucks." Many of Bargeron's schoolmates thought he was joking. Not one pupil felt obliged to report Bargeron's recruitment drive for a hitman to the school authorities.

As one of Bargeron's oldest school friends later said: "Chris had a reputation as a weirdo so none of us took much notice of him."

However it wasn't until he attended a party of tenth-graders a couple of days later that one of his fellow students mentioned a particularly off-the-wall character named Gerry Horne. Horne had virtual "hero" status because he rarely attended school and rumors had swept the school in recent months that he was hanging out with a street gang on the west side of Augusta.

Bargeron soon established that Gerry Horne had left his family home and was staying at various addresses in the area. He sounded like the perfect hitman, if Bargeron could track him down.

SIXTEEN

On Monday, May 5, 1997, Chris Bargeron got a phone call from one of Gerry Horne's friends saying that Horne was staying at a motel called the Royal Palms, on the Peach Orchard strip. The friend said he'd spoken to Horne, who had said he was interested in the "work" that Bargeron was offering.

A few hours later Bargeron met with Gerry Horne. He soon realized why Horne had a reputation amongst many of the local kids as a tough guy. He certainly talked a good fight even though few had ever seen him actually do anything bad.

The 18-year-old Horne, with his skinhead hair cut, goatee beard and sharp features, was well known on the Peach Orchard strip because of his patronage of numerous fast-food joints and motels. He booked himself into local hostelries whenever he ran out of friends' houses to stay at. Many believed that he subsidized his accommodation by selling drugs. Horne's attendance at school had become so occasional that teachers just presumed he would flunk out. Somehow he had remained on the roll, although his days were definitely numbered.

Horne was partial to the Royal Palms Motel, just

a few blocks south of Taco Bell, because it was cheap and had a back entrance that enabled him to come and go with whoever he liked without being hassled by the manager.

The Royal Palms had a reputation amongst local police and residents as a flophouse of questionable repute. Only a couple of months earlier, a hammer-wielding bandit who had held up a nearby Hardee's was arrested there in dramatic circumstances.

It was known amongst local teenagers as the kind of place where people could check in with no questions asked. For those not old enough to frequent the local bars and clubs it had become the perfect location for a party.

Chris Bargeron was impressed that Horne was staying at the Royal Palms because it meant few people would know about his activities.

The youths' attitude at that meeting was so casual, it seemed as though they were talking about swapping a few CDs rather than planning to murder a man in cold blood.

Bargeron told Horne: "There's this lady called Gina and a guy called Larry and they wanta kill Gina's husband and they've got a gun, a .38 special.

"They're lookin' for someone to kill this man. Gina wants him killed 'cause he won't leave her alone 'cause she wouldn't sleep with him no more." Bargeron stopped for a moment to examine the reaction of his young would-be hitman. Then he continued: "She reckons on collecting the insurance off of him."

Horne showed little emotional reaction to Bargeron's extraordinary request. He even gave the impression that he was used to carrying out such "work."

Horne was extremely flattered that Bargeron had come to him after a recommendation from a friend in tenth grade at Butler High.

Bargeron informed Horne he'd deliver $2,000 up front in cash when he handed over the gun. However Bargeron was most insistent that Horne ditch the weapon immediately after the killing because it had been stolen from Larry Kelley's stepfather.

Horne didn't tell Bargeron, but he preferred the idea of keeping the gun and decided he'd make that decision on the day of the killing.

Perhaps rather clumsily, Chris Bargeron admitted to Horne that Gina was going to pay him a certain sum of money but he refused to tell Horne exactly how much that would be.

Horne then laid down some of the ground rules if the deal was to go ahead. He told Bargeron he never wanted to meet either Gina or Larry and that they should never know his name.

Gerry Horne had seen enough splatter movies to know that the fewer people who knew his identity, the more chance he had of getting away with murder.

Two days later, Chris Bargeron called up Horne and said he was ready to hand over Larry Kelley's stepfather's gleaming .38 special.

Far from being the cold-blooded shooter he'd implied he was during earlier conversations with Larry and Gina, Chris Bargeron was actually a rather cautious individual. He was involved only because he believed he could make a lot of money without even getting his hands dirty.

Bargeron was so careful he made Horne come to his house because he didn't want to walk anywhere with the weapon in his pocket in case he got stopped by the police. Horne went down to Bargeron's house just off Lumpkin Road next to a Methodist church near the Peach Orchard strip. Horne was so reckless he didn't give the matter much thought.

Bargeron knew that once Horne had taken delivery of the gun there was little chance of his going back on the plan. Bargeron reminded Horne that by getting rid of the weapon as quickly as possible he would be distancing himself from the crime that had been committed. No one knows to this day if the promised $2,000 "deposit" was ever paid.

On Friday, May 9, 1997, Bargeron once again met up with Horne at his room in the Royal Palms Motel for some final discussions. Bargeron informed Horne that his client wanted the hit to be carried out as soon as possible. She also wanted her own white Toyota to be stolen as part of the cover plan. The car was a spare vehicle parked up alongside the house on Old Waynesboro. The conversation that evolved was bizarre, to say the least:

"I got a car for you to take. It's a manual stick-shift," Bargeron informed Horne, expecting him to be pleased.

"I can't use it. I want an automatic. I gotta have an automatic."

"Gina won't leave the automatic 'cause it's her new car."

Horne was infuriated. He didn't want to admit he couldn't drive a stick-shift.

Horne later insisted that what he really meant was that he didn't seriously intend to kill anyone and the disagreement about a stick-shift was just his way of trying to get out of the deal.

Whatever the truth of the matter, Horne's half-hearted attempt to wriggle out of killing a man was then interrupted by a knock at the door of room 20 at the Royal Palms Motel. It was one of Horne's friends, 16-year-old Matt Piazzi.

Instead of telling his young friend to go away, Horne invited him in and immediately involved him in the conversation. Chris Bargeron was surprised because he'd been under the impression that the fewer people who knew about the intended hit the better.

What Bargeron didn't realize was that, despite being younger than Horne, Matt Piazzi was held in high esteem by his older friend. The teenager had impressed Horne by claiming that he'd killed a man when he and his family had lived in South Carolina. Horne was feeling nervous about what he'd agreed to do and needed some support.

With his floppy brown hair, and standing only five feet three inches, Piazzi looked like an innocent schoolboy rather than a hitman. But the teenager was so excited by what he heard that he immediately insisted he wanted to help his friend Horne carry out the hit.

Chris Bargeron did not argue with them. His priority was to ensure that the job went ahead so he could collect the cash.

*   *   *

Young Matt Piazzi's lack of effort at nearby Hephzibah High had culminated in his being advised to leave the school in the first semester of ninth grade. He had been having home school during the previous six months.

Piazzi's father Richard had been concerned for months about the company Matt was keeping. He was particularly worried about his son's friendship with Gerry Horne.

He explained: "I'd seen him hanging out with Horne and I'd told him I didn't want him hanging around him and others because I didn't like the way they looked."

But like most teenagers, Matt Piazzi chose to ignore his father's advice. And those who knew Horne and Piazzi confirmed that it was Piazzi who was the stronger of the two characters despite the two-year age difference.

Back at the Royal Palms Motel, Chris Bargeron continued briefing his two would-be hitmen. He reiterated that it would be best if they got the job done as soon as possible and suggested they go ahead that very evening.

Horne was appalled at the suggestion because he had certain other priorities.

"Hey, man, I got a party over here tonight. Lots of chicks, booze and dope. I can't cancel at short notice."

Horne later claimed that he gave Bargeron this excuse because he didn't really want to go through with the hit and was putting up barriers against it all the time.

Bargeron sensed that Horne was back-tracking and turned to loose cannon Matt Piazzi who seemed far more determined than his friend to carry out the hit.

Piazzi assured Bargeron that the hit would go through but that Bargeron had to respect Horne's decision not to do it that night.

Matt Piazzi seemed to be taking over as the main man.

Bargeron was confused by the change of personnel and the attitude of both teenagers.

In the words of Gerry Horne, Bargeron then "started acting real funny."

Neither youth ever properly elaborated on exactly what this meant. But Horne later claimed that Bargeron's behavior further discouraged him from going through with the murder of Kevin Spann.

He even said to Bargeron: "I don't like the way this thing is going."

Horne insists he then said: "I'm not gonna do it."

Chris Bargeron sensed problems but he never thought they'd actually back out of the deal. There was mention of the $2,000 not being handed over. Horne and Piazzi looked at each other. They needed their share of the cash as much as Bargeron wanted the majority of the money.

For a few seconds the three teenagers looked at each other without saying a word. They'd reached a crossroads. Someone had to make a decision.

That was when Chris Bargeron left the room and headed for a pay phone where he called Gina and told her what was happening. Gina immediately moved into "Mother" mode.

Minutes later she called Horne's room at the Royal Palms.

As Horne later recalled: "I don't know how she knew to call my room but she got through. S'ppose Chris must have told her where I was at but that was not supposed to be done either. We weren't s'pposed to talk to her."

Gina Spann was so careful not to upset her young hit team that when Horne answered the phone in the room she simply asked to speak to Chris Bargeron rather than acknowledging who Horne was.

Horne handed Chris Bargeron the phone.

"It's for you. Make it quick. I don't want no one talkin' 'bout this over the phone."

The conversation between Chris and Gina was brief and moments after putting down the receiver, Bargeron told Horne that she was driving over to the motel to see him.

Horne was furious. All the procedures and precautions he'd talked about earlier had been completely discarded.

"I can't talk to her in person, man," a tense Horne told Bargeron. "She mustn't see my face and I can't go ridin' in her car neither."

Then as an afterthought Horne threw in: "And I'm not takin' that car. I want an automatic. That's the deal or I'm not doin' it."

That was when his pint-sized friend Matt Piazzi chipped in: "I can drive it. Gimme a Magnum, I'll drive that." Piazzi was so proud of his familiarity with guns he couldn't resist mentioning them even when they were talking about a stick-shift car.

Horne felt that Piazzi was undermining him in

front of Bargeron. He was actually more concerned with this humiliation than with the fact that he was about to make a final commitment to killing a man.

Horne barked back: "I can, too, but that's not the fuckin' point, man."

Gina's Toyota was not meant as a payment for the would-be killers. It was supposed to provide transport for the two youths to flee the area so that police would get the impression that the motive behind the killing was theft. The killers were to dump the car and page Gina once their mission had been accomplished.

Having ironed out the wrinkles, Chris called Gina back and told her not to come to the motel. He assured her that the plan was going ahead, after all.

The three youths decided on a reluctant truce. The hit was finalized but Horne reiterated that it would have to wait until the following night.

Chris Bargeron and the others sat in nervous silence for a few minutes in Gerry Horne's motel room. Horne took out Larry Kelley's stepfather's .38 and the five bullets it came with, and began polishing it. He panned it around the room, laughing. Then he stroked it. Then he spun the empty chamber and laughed out loud. At last he seemed to have the taste for murder.

By the time Chris Bargeron left Gerry Horne's motel room early that evening of Friday, May 9, 1997, he was confident that the plan to kill Kevin Spann was again on course.

He'd had certain reservations about Horne and Piazzi but the moment he'd seen Horne nursing that .38 he reckoned they'd go through with it.

Bargeron decided to get out of the motel room before Horne's party started later that evening. He wanted to continue keeping a distance between himself and the would-be killers.

He believed that within twenty-four hours, Kevin Spann would finally be dead and he could collect his money.

On the Peach Orchard strip, Gerry Horne certainly had a bit of a reputation. Gina Spann's Taco Bell co-worker Amanda Quick had an older sister named Shanna who remembered Gerry Horne as a trouble-maker.

"Gerry didn't work. He just took drugs all day long. Anything he could get his hands on. I heard that he liked crack and all those boys smoked weed 'til it came outta their ears. I made a point of keepin' well away from them."

Gerry Horne had also been in trouble with the law. Recalled Shanna Quick: "He wasn't the kind of guy you wanted to hang out with much. Most other kids' parents didn't even want him in their homes."

Ironically, Matt Piazzi's family had a completely different reputation. Shanna described it: "Matt had four brothers and sisters. A real regular family. They never allowed drink or drugs in the house. Matt was quite a sensitive type of guy. I was surprised he didn't have a girlfriend 'cause he was so cute-lookin'."

Back at the house on Old Waynesboro that Friday evening, Gina Spann had grown increasingly agitated despite Chris Bargeron's reassurances.

What none of the youths realized was that Gina had another reason for feeling irritated and emotionally drained; Mother's Day was less than two days away.

Gina had been feeling under so much pressure from the impending day of celebration that she even went to a doctor to get some medication to try and offset the inevitable depression that Mother's Day brought with it.

The day was building and building in her mind and she hoped that the murder of her husband would obliterate all the painful memories of Mother's Day from her life forever.

SEVENTEEN

On Saturday, May 10, 1997, Gina Spann woke after a restless night and spent more than an hour tracking down Chris Bargeron. She finally got him on the phone and told him she wanted the hit on her husband to be carried out that night—otherwise she'd cancel the entire operation.

Bargeron told her that was the plan. But just to make sure it all went ahead, later that afternoon he headed over to the Royal Palms Motel and informed Gerry Horne that his client was piling on the pressure.

Horne was irritated by Bargeron waking him up to go over the plan, when he thought they'd finalized the entire scheme the previous evening. He'd only gotten to bed at 7 A.M. after partying all night.

"We gotta talk this plan through—make sure it works," Bargeron told Horne.

Then Bargeron started discussing plans different from the one agreed upon the night before. It confused Horne and he started to get nervous about the murder plot.

"I don't like the way this is goin'," Horne told Bargeron. Then he broke his own iron-clad rule. "I need to talk to one of them," he said.

Bargeron was confused because up until that point Horne had been insisting that there be no contact with Gina or Larry.

Bargeron left the room at the Royal Palms and headed across the busy Peach Orchard strip to a pay phone next to a fast-food joint.

A few minutes later Bargeron returned to room 20 and told Horne that Gina would be over in ten minutes to talk to them and then take them on their assignment. This time there really was no turning back.

Any hesitation Horne might have felt was overridden by Bargeron's concrete attitude.

Meanwhile, Matt Piazzi sounded positively upbeat about the prospect of murdering someone in cold blood. He was the driving force behind it all now, or so it seemed.

When Gina Spann turned up at the Royal Palms Motel she was in an irritable mood. She told them that they had to steal the car from outside the house before they went back to commit the hit because then they'd have their own transport. The ever-enthusiastic Matt Piazzi immediately volunteered to go with Gina Spann to get the white stick-shift Toyota.

Less than half an hour later, Piazzi propelled the Toyota up to the rear parking lot of the Royal Palms. Stage one of the plan had been achieved with relative ease.

But Horne had been thinking while his friend was out with Gina collecting the car. He was extremely nervous about the planned hit and feared that he was being swept up by the others. Within minutes of their return, Horne announced that he and Piazzi had to go out to get some gloves for them to wear while carrying out the hit.

In fact Horne and Piazzi went over to a friend's house a couple of blocks away because Horne wanted to completely re-think the plan and he did not want to discuss it in front of Gina and Chris.

While they were out, some of Horne's other friends showed up at the motel.

Shanna Quick knew all about the plan to kill Kevin Spann because she'd dated a youth who spent a lot of time hanging out with Horne and Piazzi. On that same Saturday, May 10, this youth had spent much of the day with them.

He later told Shanna Quick that he also spent some of that Saturday night at the Royal Palms Motel with Gina Spann and the others. "He reckoned they did some weed and crack together. I think maybe there mighta been some other drugs, too," she recalled.

The youth even made a strange phone call to Shanna that night. "He made out that Matt and Gerry were real serious about doing something but he didn't say what they were going to do," said Shanna, who then decided to try and get to the bottom of what was going on.

"Is that why you're hanging out together?" she asked the youth.

"Yeah. It's cool, baby."

She later recalled: "I could tell [he] was high but I wanted to know more so I asked him."

"Why'd you go down to that hotel and meet them?"

"We're gonna get some money for what we do."

*   *   *

Amanda Quick was over at her friend Bobby Joe's house just a couple of blocks from the Peach Orchard strip when Gerry Horne and Matt Piazzi turned up at the front door having told Gina that they were going out to get some gloves. It soon became clear to Amanda and her friends that Piazzi and Horne were planning something.

At first the two youths remained uncharacteristically quiet. Amanda and the others presumed they were high on drugs although they weren't doing anything particularly crazy. However, they did seem nervous and kept pacing around the house.

Then the two youths walked out into the back yard and began whispering to each other. Amanda couldn't hear what they were talking about but it was obviously "something, like, real secretive."

Back inside the house some of the other youths present seemed to have an idea what was going on.

One said: "Gerry and Matt been bullshittin' about doing some hit or something."

The others laughed.

When Piazzi and Horne came back in the house they were still talking but no one was near enough to hear what they were saying.

Gerry and Matt hung out at the house for about an hour in all. They had a couple of beers before announcing that they had to leave to meet someone at the Royal Palms Motel.

Amanda's friend Bobby Joe offered to drive them up there in his Oldsmobile. "They didn't have no wheels so we felt kinda sorry for them," recalled Amanda.

Five minutes later, Amanda, Bobby Joe and the

two youths rolled up at the back entrance to the Royal Palms Motel.

Amanda needed to use the bathroom so she went up to the room with the two boys. As she walked in she immediately noticed that everyone looked as if they were wired on drugs. Then she noticed Gina Spann chopping out some white powder on a mirror.

Amanda ignored it and used the bathroom. But as she left she also noticed some marijuana in a plastic bag on the bed. Gina was still busy chopping up that powder.

As Amanda was opening the door to leave she turned and looked directly at Gerry Horne, who was sitting in a chair by the window.

He had a gun in his hand. He was nursing it, stroking it very proudly. He smiled when he saw Amanda looking at the weapon. She looked away as if she hadn't really noticed but he knew she'd seen it. It was then that she realized something very dangerous was about to happen.

On the way back to Amanda's house, Bobby Joe told her that Horne and Piazzi were going to shoot someone for some insurance money. "I laughed about it 'cause it seemed kinda dumb. Like something out of the movies, I guess," recalled Amanda. "I didn't really know they were serious."

Not one of them considered calling the police . . .

Gina Spann departed from the Royal Palms Motel with Larry Kelley shortly after Amanda Quick. She was under the impression that the job she had commissioned was finally about to be carried out.

Horne and Piazzi then left Chris Bargeron in the

motel room and headed for the Toyota in the parking lot. They later claimed that Chris Bargeron had wanted to go with them but they told him to stay in the room. They didn't want anyone just along for the ride.

Horne had the .38 in his pocket and Piazzi was rather excited about the prospect of having a free car to use.

Piazzi turned the Toyota south on the Peach Orchard strip and began the short drive to the Spann house.

Ten minutes later Piazzi and Horne pulled up in the driveway to the house. It was 12:30 a.m. on Sunday, May 11, 1997. *Mother's Day*.

The two youths cut the car's engine, got out, looked around and then walked up to the front door. They peered in the windows and then moved around to the back of the house. The back door was open and they could see into the den, so they walked in.

Matt Piazzi stepped in first and moved as far as the kitchen. Then he came back towards Horne.

That was when Horne thought he heard someone talking on the phone.

He whispered to Piazzi: "Go get in the car and crank it up."

Horne then walked further into the house and listened for any more sounds. All he could hear was a radio so he moved on down the hallway a few feet.

Horne later recalled: "I didn't see anyone or anything or hear anything except for the radio."

Horne turned around and walked back out of the house and went around to the side of the house where the car was parked.

He leaned in to Piazzi in the driver's seat of the Toyota: "Get ready to go."

Then Horne walked around to the front between the trees in the front yard and fired a shot at the house next to a side window.

He later insisted it had been a warning shot to let their intended victim know that someone was trying to kill him. Horne insisted he had no intention of going through with the killing.

Then Horne jumped in the white Toyota and Matt Piazzi drove them back up Old Waynesboro Road at a leisurely pace so as not to cause too much attention. He need not have bothered.

Less than a minute later, Horne opened the window and started waving the gleaming .38 around as they cruised up the dimly lit street.

"Pull over," shouted Horne.

"What?"

"Pull over."

"Why?"

"Just do it."

Piazzi pulled the car up outside a darkened house about a quarter of a mile from the Spann home.

Horne lifted the pistol and took aim.

"You fuckin' crazy?" screamed Piazzi.

Horne ignored him and pulled the trigger. After the bang there was a smashing of a window pane.

Piazzi put his foot to the floor and the old white Toyota screeched off up the road.

Horne was still waving the gun around like a demented cowboy when they reached the junction with Highway 53.

EIGHTEEN

Matt Piazzi and Gerry Horne were supposed to page Gina Spann after they'd killed her husband and she was then going to report the Toyota stolen.

But having failed to carry out the job, the two teen-agers had other plans for that free car. They picked up Horne's girlfriend and then Piazzi's and headed back to Horne's room at the Royal Palms Motel where they intended to stay the remainder of that night.

Both youths deliberately didn't page Gina because they knew she would have then reported the car stolen and Matt Piazzi still wanted to use it.

But not everything went their way. Back at the Royal Palms Motel, Piazzi had a bust-up with his girl-friend and stormed off in the Toyota.

Piazzi drove the car up to a friend's house, went in and drank a few beers with his pals. He told them what he and Horne had tried to do that night and openly bragged to his friends that they'd probably give it another shot the following night.

Then he headed off in the white Toyota once more.

Kevin Spann didn't call the police himself following the shooting incident outside his house because he thought the shot had been a car backfiring. It was a neighbor's 911 call which eventually brought a visit from a deputy in a Richmond County sheriff's black-and-silver cruiser.

Kevin Spann's own recollection of what happened at approximately 12:30 A.M. completely overlooked the reality of the situation.

He told the deputy: "I got out of the tub to investigate. And as I was heading out front I did hear a vehicle leaving and it could have been one of ours.

"Moments later I discovered that our '86 Toyota was missing from the driveway. I thought Gina musta taken it. I think Gina owns it although it doesn't get driven that often. The car doesn't have any insurance but we start it occasionally to keep the batteries charging."

Kevin even light-heartedly told officers that he reckoned his wife Gina had probably left the keys in the vehicle the last time she started it.

But then Kevin discovered that $200 in cash and his Wachovia bank ATM card were missing from his wallet.

The police were mystified because they couldn't find any sign of a forced entry into the residence.

A few hours later Kevin made a much more ominous discovery and called up the Augusta Police.

"You know what? I found a bullet hole in my son's bedroom window."

That bullet had actually passed through the window and left a hole in the facing on a chest of drawers in young Michael's room.

When police arrived back at the house they couldn't find the bullet. As Kevin Spann told one investigator at the time: "It wasn't that surprising since Mike's room was so trashed."

What Kevin Spann didn't realize was that a few minutes after the shooting Gina had silently crept into the house and been so surprised to find her husband still alive that she immediately went back to her car and headed out into the night.

Unable to sleep after an evening of drug-taking, Gina and Larry decided to get some sodas. Gina drove by a garage called Western Auto and immediately noticed her white Toyota, which she had gotten Piazzi to steal just a few hours earlier. It was parked up on a side-street.

Gina was tempted to stop and look at the vehicle but resisted in case there were any police in the area. Five minutes later she rode by and the car had disappeared.

Gina was extremely agitated as she pulled out onto Lumpkin Avenue and then went on to make a left-hand turn onto the Peach Orchard strip. Suddenly the very same Toyota pulled up behind her. Matt Piazzi was at the wheel.

Gina stuck her hand out the window and pointed to the side of the road. The two cars made a turn and Piazzi pulled up beside Gina.

"What the fuck are you doin'? Get rid of the car now. The cops will know it's been stolen," barked Gina.

Piazzi tried to explain that he'd kept the car because he intended to drive back to the house on Old Waynesboro and find the bullet they had fired earlier.

"What's this bullshit looking for the bullet?" she asked Piazzi.

"I don't know where the bullet went. We gotta find it."

But Gina had other priorities.

"They're looking for the car. You need to ditch the fucking car."

Piazzi then got very aggressive with Gina and warned her about Gerry Horne and how his family were gangsters and how they could cause her problems.

Gina even admitted later: "That just kinda fucked me up."

Piazzi then mentioned Chris Bargeron and how he and Gerry Horne were so angry at Bargeron that they wanted to kill him.

Gina Spann should have taken a step back and abandoned her plan there and then. But she couldn't stop thinking about that insurance money and what a great life she would have once Kevin was dead.

She ordered Piazzi to dump the car and head back to the Royal Palms Motel where she would meet them later that day.

Gina was so worried about what so-called hitman Piazzi had said about killing Chris Bargeron that she called him at his home to warn him.

"They're pissed off. You need to stay away from them," whispered Gina into the phone. Then she told him she'd come by later to discuss a plan.

One of Bargeron's school friends later explained: "Chris was so freaked out he started talking about going to Florida."

*　　*　　*

Over at the family home of Matt Piazzi on South Atlantic Drive, his mother Kathy was getting extremely worried about where her son was. He'd been missing for four days and had promised her he would come home and cut the lawn as a Mother's Day gift.

Kathy grew so concerned by the middle of that Sunday she contacted the local police and filed a missing persons report. She pointed out that despite being so young it was not unusual for her son to be missing for days at a time.

She even admitted to police that Matt had run away from home on several occasions in the past following fights with her. But she also said that the last time she had spoken to him was three days earlier and she was very concerned about his safety.

While Mrs. Piazzi fretted about her son, Gerry Horne and Matt Piazzi spent much of Mother's Day either asleep or watching TV in their room at the Royal Palms.

Over at the Spanns' house, Gina was growing increasingly angry about their failure to kill her husband. The Mother's Day celebrations going on all around her simply compounded her fury.

That evening, Gina called Gerry Horne from a gas station near the motel. She was not happy.

"We need to talk," she told Horne.

"Come over and talk to me in person. Don't, don't talk over my phone. Where are you?"

"Across the street at the BP."

"See you in five."

So Gina walked across the busy Peach Orchard strip with Larry Kelley. They arrived at about nine o'clock.

Horne, Piazzi and a friend were in the room.

Gina turned on Horne. "Personally, I think you're fucking with me, bud."

"No I didn't fuck with you," replied Horne.

Gina told the youths that she'd specially drugged her husband and he'd passed out in the bathtub, perfectly primed to be hit by the triggerman. It was all a lie deliberately manufactured to put them under even more pressure.

"It was the perfect moment. What happened? You got no balls?" snapped Gina.

"He fired from the yard so he didn't have much chance of hittin' the target," volunteered Piazzi.

Gina snapped back: "Well, I want it done right or you're not gettin' your money."

Gina paused for breath.

"I'd do it myself but I have to have an alibi and the gunpowder burns would give me away. I gotta have someone else do it," said Gina. "But I don't want no more of this shittin' around. You understand?"

She continued: "I been trying to kill him for a year. I want him dead. *Now!*"

She wasn't finished. "If you're gonna do it then do it," She looked across at her young lover. "Larry hasn't got the balls to do it."

Matt Piazzi interrupted: "I'll do it."

Horne hesitated, then spoke up. "I'll go with him and we'll take care of it."

Gina seemed much happier. "I'll drive you up there and give you the money for a cab and you come back here and page me. Put 666 in the pager. That means it's done."

Gina told her two teenage hitmen that it would take two or three days for her to get them the money. She also told them: "I'm goin' to Chris Bargeron's house to tell him to stay away from me and to stay away from the deal or I'll kill him myself."

Horne and Piazzi were surprised by her vicious tone. Then she explained: "He was the one s'pposed to be doin' the job."

Bargeron was now being distanced from the entire scheme even though only a week previously he'd supposedly been the triggerman who was going to snuff out Kevin Spann's life and make his widow an extremely rich woman.

"Right. Let's go," barked Gina, who was back in her finest "Mother" mode.

NINETEEN

Gina dropped Gerry Horne and Matt Piazzi off on Covington Road and gave them ten dollars for a cab ride once they'd carried out the hit on Kevin Spann. It was 9:30 P.M. on Mother's Day 1997.

Gina was mothering those boys right up to that point. She treated them more like children than hired killers.

The two youths stood on the corner and watched Gina rev up the engine of her Cavalier and drive off. Gerry Horne wore a white shirt with the words *The Ultimate Guy* emblazoned across the chest. He really did believe that was what he was.

They waited for her to disappear around the corner before setting out for 3805 Old Waynesboro Road.

As they walked up the deserted street, Gerry passed the .38 special to his friend.

"It's only got three bullets so don't go wastin' any," said Horne. "All you have to do is pull the hammer back on it and point it and pull the trigger."

Matt replied: "I know how to do it." Then he reminded his friend: "I shot some dude before, you know."

As Horne later recalled: "I don't know to this day

if he was shittin' me or what. But he sounded real serious about it."

Meanwhile Gina went home and picked up her son Michael. She didn't want him in the house if there were bullets flying around.

Gina then pulled out of the driveway with Larry and Michael. She headed back past the intersection where she'd dropped the boys earlier. There was no sign of them so she presumed they were heading for the house.

At 10:15 P.M. Gina, her son and her lover arrived at Chris Bargeron's house on Fernwood Circle. Gina immediately asked Bargeron to call the Royal Palms Motel to see if they were back.

Gina later claimed: "I wanted to say, 'Let's not do this shit,' because I was starting to get scared and I didn't want to . . . but they weren't there. No one answered the phone."

So Gina and her entourage went and got something to eat before heading back home.

The headlights of a truck swept around the corner from a side street. Piazzi and Horne immediately ducked into the bushes by the side of 3805 Old Waynesboro Road so they wouldn't be caught in the full beams.

Seconds after the throbbing V-8 moved past them they moved back up to the front door. Piazzi cocked the gun. His friend knocked on the door and they waited. And waited. And waited.

The .38 caliber nickel-plated Taurus with a 3-inch barrel and black Pachmeye grips was loaded with three blue-tip ball-type bullets. It felt cold in Matt

Piazzi's hand. He gripped the gun tightly and panned it around for a few moments just like he'd seen them do in the movies and on TV.

"Come on," said Horne.

Then Horne knocked again.

There was still no reply.

Horne tried again. This time much harder. The two youths heard movement inside the house, followed by the shuffling of feet towards the other side of the front door.

Piazzi's grip on the gun tightened. He was so tense he started to worry that he might pull the trigger before it was time.

Then the latch inside the front door snapped and it opened gently. Bleary-eyed Kevin Spann, in a T-shirt and jeans, stood in front of the boys.

"Gina and Larry here?" asked Matt.

"They're out someplace . . ." replied Kevin Spann.

Piazzi's finger squeezed tight. The gun went off from such close range that Kevin Spann didn't even change the expression on his face.

As Piazzi later told one investigator proudly: "I shot the motherfucker. *Pow!*"

The first bullet entered Kevin Spann's cheek and burst through his brain, killing him instantly.

Horne recounted: "That's when I heard the first, the first shot go off and then I heard the man hit the floor."

Kevin Spann's life had already been snuffed out when Piazzi fired a second shot for good measure. That bullet tore through Kevin's throat and exited out his back.

Horne continued: "I could hear him like choking

on blood and I heard another shot and it was quiet."

The two youths stood there in deathly silence for a few beats. They looked down at their victim and their eyes snapped around in all directions.

Then Horne hollered: "Come on!"

The pair moved briskly back across the front yard to the main road that ran in front of the house. Then they began walking back down towards Covington and the highway beyond.

Neighbor Joe Martin was never much of a heavy sleeper so when he heard two bangs and then his dog began barking wildly well before midnight on Sunday, May 11, 1997 he decided to get up and investigate.

His house on Covington Drive was just a few hundred yards from the Spanns' residence.

At first Joe just assumed that someone had slapped the stop sign in front of his house. But when his dog didn't stop barking in the back yard he got out of bed.

As Joe Martin emerged onto his front porch, Matt Piazzi and Gerry Horne walked by.

Horne immediately noticed the man watching them.

And as Joe Martin later recalled: "They were a strange-lookin' pair to be out so late. One of them was short and looked real young."

Joe Martin watched the two youths walk down the road past the front of his house. He noticed they kept looking behind themselves.

He continued watching them as they moved towards the wooded area out in the direction of Forward Augusta. Joe Martin stepped back into his house. As he later explained: "I didn't think much of it and went back inside and went back to sleep."

A few hundred yards farther up the street Matt Piazzi and Gerry Horne began, in the words of Matt, "to pretty much hauling ass" as they stepped up the tempo and moved swiftly across the road, into fields and towards a local wood to try and put as much distance as they could between themselves and the cold-blooded crime they had just committed.

They scrambled through a set of back yards and moved onto a residential road next to a huge power plant that was spookily gushing out gray smoke illuminated by the moonlight.

Then as the two youths moved across one shadowy back yard a dog growled. It sounded frighteningly close. As they turned a corner they found themselves face to face with a Rottweiler, baring its teeth and waiting to pounce. Piazzi went even paler than he had been a few moments earlier as they stood rooted to the ground too terrified to move.

Just then the Rottweiler leapt at them both. They moved back and realized the animal was on a chain and he was straining to get any closer than one foot from them. The two youths speedily headed off towards the nearby fields.

As they crossed through a small wood, Piazzi silently pulled the .38 out of his jacket and threw it into a row of bushes. Gerry Horne never had a chance to say that he'd been thinking of keeping the gun. Both youths were so hyped up by the adrenaline that they couldn't think straight. Their only aim was to keep moving.

Eventually, they got through the wood and burst onto Tobacco Road panting and sweating. Faced with a public road and back to familiar surroundings, Piazzi and Horne stopped running and began walking at a normal pace up the deserted highway.

A few hundred yards later they got to a pay phone and called a cab.

"We wanna go to Ryan's Steakhouse," Piazzi told the cab company operator.

"Kinda late for dinner, ain't it?" replied the operator.

It was still forty minutes before the end of Mother's Day 1997.

On the way home from Chris Bargeron's house, Gina, Michael and Larry decided to head to a Crown gas station to pick up some sodas.

As Gina's headlights swept into the forecourt they illuminated the two youths who'd just murdered her husband sitting next to the pay phone on the curb out by the road.

Gina pulled her car around to the other side of the forecourt. For a few moments she sat and thought about her next move. She could ignore them and hope they'd page her later with the news or she could take a chance and talk to them there and then.

Gina told Michael and Larry to wait in the car, then took a deep breath and got out. She walked slowly towards Gerry Horne.

She was still unsure if this was going to turn out to be the biggest mistake of her life.

Horne got up and looked completely unfazed by

Gina's appearance. He even smiled gently as he told her: "He's dead now. He's 666."

As Horne later recalled: "They didn't even know that we'd be there, which was kinda freaky."

Matt Piazzi jumped up hyperactively. "I shot him," he said. "I shot him twice. Don't walk in the door, else you'll find him."

Gina later claimed she didn't believe them.

"You're fucking around, right?"

They didn't reply.

She didn't say anything for a moment, then: "Well, I gotta go. I can't be seen talkin' to y'all."

Gina hurried back to her car.

Cab driver Ed McKowski pulled up his vehicle as Horne and Piazzi approached.

They told him they wanted to go to Ryan's Steakhouse on Peach Orchard Road.

As they got into the cab one of them turned to the driver and said: "It's gonna be about six dollars?"

McKowski shook his head slowly and sighed quietly.

"It'll be more than that. That gonna be a problem?"

Horne replied: "No problem."

As the cab moved up the Peach Orchard strip, McKowski mentioned to the youths that the restaurant would be closed.

"We're going to a friend's house across the street from there," responded Horne.

As Ed McKowski pulled up at the restaurant he noticed an African American woman leaning against a wall smoking a cigarette. His recollection of that night was very precise.

"That'll be nine dollars."

Horne handed the driver a ten-dollar bill.

"Keep the change."

As McKowski drove off he noticed the two youths walking north along the strip on the same side of the road as the restaurant. He later recalled: "I never did see them crossing the road like they said they were going to."

TWENTY

Gerry Horne and Matt Piazzi got the cab to drop them by the steakhouse because it was near the Royal Palms Motel. But they didn't want the driver to know they were staying there. They got back to room 20 at 11:30 P.M.

Horne later insisted that he paged Gina Spann twice from his room but she never called back. Why he would still page her when they'd already seen her was not clear.

Despite the fact that they'd just shot a man to death in cold blood Horne and Piazzi were relatively calm by the time they got back to the motel.

Horne even found time to ask Piazzi about the other murder he'd earlier claimed he'd been involved in.

"I shot the guy once in the chest and then twice more in the face with a .45 I owned," Piazzi replied in a remarkably cool manner.

Soon afterwards, both of them fell asleep on their beds with the TV blaring in front of them. It had been a long day and night.

*   *   *

A few minutes later Gina, Michael and Larry pulled into their back yard beside her husband's Ford Mustang.

Michael and Larry immediately raced around the pool that Kevin had bought a few months earlier. They were behaving more like teenage brothers than son and part-time stepfather.

The two boys then headed for the back den of the house and sat down with a six-pack of sodas and two videos which they intended to watch.

Meanwhile Gina Spann moved towards the front of the house. She'd already noticed that the front door seemed to be open. She walked with slight trepidation, unsure if she really wanted to find out what had happened.

As she entered the front room area she saw Kevin Spann's corpse crumpled on the carpeted floor. Blood was pouring from the head wound. He was still and she knew the moment she looked at him that he was dead.

The front door remained wide open and every now and again a car sped past, blissfully unaware of the tragedy that had just unfolded a few yards away. The cars' headlights cast a strong yellow light across the front room followed by pitch black.

Gina Spann leaned down to touch him. There was no response but she wanted to be sure nothing could be done. She even called out to him, "Kevin? Kevin?"

Nothing.

She ran back to the den and shouted at her teenage lover and young son.

"Get outta here. *Now*!"

"Why?" responded Larry.

"Just get the fuck outta here," said Gina.

Larry pulled Michael with him and they got into the Cavalier.

A few moments later Gina joined them and they traveled to a pay phone next to a store called Johnson's just a quarter of a mile from the house.

This is a police transcription of that conversation:

911:      911.

Spann: I need, uh, I, I please, I really need a ambulance at 3805 . . .

911:      What's your problem?

Spann: I need an ambulance.

911:      Okay, what's your problem?

Spann: He's got blood everywhere. I don't know. I just walked in and there's blood everywhere.

911:      Okay, what's that address?

Spann: 3805 Old Waynesboro Road.

911:      You can't tell what happened?

Spann: I just walked in the door and there's blood everywhere and I took my son and I throw him in the car and I came to a pay phone.

911:      Hold on for me. Steve, can you pick up on seven?

Steve: Channel seven.

911:      Give him your information, ma'am, okay?

Steve: Hello?

Spann: Hello.

Steve: Yes, ma'am. What's the problem?

Spann: I need, I need an ambulance.

Steve: Okay, ma'am. What's the problem?

Spann: I don't know. I went in the door and there's blood everywhere. My husband's on the floor.

Steve: What, your husband's on the floor?

Spann: And there's blood everywhere.

Steve: Okay, is he breathing?

Spann: I don't know. I don't think so.

Steve: You guys en route?

911:    Uh huh.

Steve: All right.

911:    Ma'am, is this a trailer or, or a house or what did you say?

Spann: It's a house.

911:    Okay, the 3805?

Spann: Yes.

911:    Okay, we're trying to get someone en route.

Spann: (Unintelligible).

911:    Are you, you, you on the phone, in a phone booth?

Spann: What?

911:    Are you in a phone booth?

Spann: Yes.

911:    Okay, okay . . .

Steve: What, what's the actual address?

Spann: 3805.

911:    Get somebody out there at 3805. Her husband's laying on the floor and she says blood is everywhere.

Steve: Okay.

911:    Breathing unknown.

Steve: Is it a house or a trailer, ma'am?

Spann: It's a house.

Steve: It's a house?

Spann: House.

Steve: Okay. I'm going to stay on the, I'm going to stay on the line with you.

911:   Get someone out to that Waynesboro Road. Lady on the phone says she walked in and blood was everywhere and her husband is on the floor and she don't know what's wrong with him.

(?):   (Unintelligible).

911:   Old Waynesboro Road.

Steve: Are you pumping already?

911:   Huh?

Steve: (Unintelligible) four, twenty-three.

911:   Okay, so you just left out, ma'am? You didn't check him or anything?

Spann: I tried to move him. I tried to wake him up and he wouldn't move.

911:   He wouldn't wake up?

Spann: No.

911:   Okay. Did you see any entry wound. you know like . . .

Spann: I couldn't hear you.

911:   Did you see, you know, was he shot or stabbed . . .

Spann: (Unintelligible).

911:   Huh?

Spann: There's just blood everywhere . . .

911:   There was blood everywhere?

Spann: I (unintelligible).

911:     Was the door locked when you got there?

Spann: The door was, the front door was open. I couldn't see the back door when I was in the living room. The front door was open and he was laying on the floor.

911:     The front door was open?

Spann: Yes.

911:     Okay. We're trying to get someone out there, okay?

Spann: (Unintelligible).

911:     How far are you from home?

Spann: Only a block.

911:     A block? Can you get home?

Spann: Yes.

911:     Huh?

Spann: Yes.

911:     Okay, you just stay on the phone with us and you just watch out for the police, okay?

Spann: Okay.

911:     Stay on the phone.

Spann: Okay. (Unintelligible).

911:     Huh?

Spann: (Unintelligible). Can I go home?

911:     Do you want to go back there?

Spann: I don't know. I don't know what I want to do.

911:     If you want to, ma'am, you can go back there.

Spann: (Unintelligible).

911:     Okay.

(?):   She needs to stay outside . . .

911:        She can, she can see her house from there.

Spann: (Unintelligible).

911:        Okay, just, just stay on the phone . . .

Spann: The police . . .

911:        The policeman's there?

Spann: A police is there.

911:        He is there? She say the police is there, Kathy, that's why. Okay, all right.

Spann: Can I go?

911:        Just meet the police, okay?

Spann: Okay.

911:        All right, good-bye.

TWENTY-ONE

May 11, 1997—Mother's Day—had been a warm day in Augusta. Richmond County police investigator Jimmy Vowell even made a point of dropping by his own mother's house before starting the late shift that day. His marriage had broken up some years previously so he particularly liked to make a special effort with his mom.

Vowell was a dependable, down-to-earth detective with a dry take on life. The kind of person who takes things in his stride.

At thirty-seven years of age and with sixteen years in the Richmond County Sheriff's Department he thought he'd seen just about everything. Vowell had started in the uniform division before moving into traffic dealing with DUI's and speed radar on the freeways. "It was run-of-the-mill but it's what you gotta do to understand this job."

Then in 1992 Vowell was promoted out of uniform to become a burglary investigator. A couple of years later he moved into dealing with violent crimes. As he later said: "That's when this job became real interesting."

Up until May of 1997, the biggest case Jimmy

Vowell had ever handled was when a well-liked Augusta school principal was murdered by her daughter. "It was all over a delinquent $1500 Visa card bill," Vowell later explained. "The mother had gotten a call from the Visa people a couple of days earlier and called up her daughter to complain. When the daughter turned up at her mother's house they got into a struggle and she killed her mom. It was kinda sad, tragic—a real waste of a life."

At 10:46 P.M. on that Mother's Day Sunday evening Jimmy Vowell received a signal 10 call on his car radio as he drove through West Augusta. Signal 10 meant a gunshot victim was down.

Vowell immediately called the deputy at the scene who told him a dead man had been found in the doorway of his home at 3805 Old Waynesboro Road, in south Richmond County.

"Maintain the crime scene and don't let anyone in but the EMT [emergency medical technicians] guys. And make sure you close it off. We'll be there as soon as we can," Vowell told the deputy.

He then radioed his partner Bobby Williams, who was in another Q car, and they traveled at high speed across town. Vowell was driving his favorite green Crown Victoria that night. It was a good, clean, reliable vehicle and he always tried to pick it out of the pool.

By the time Vowell arrived at the Spann house a few minutes after 11 P.M., yellow crime-scene tape was already up around the yard perimeter of the property. The lights of three black-and-silver Augusta Police Department cruisers and an ambulance cast a flickering red shadow across the property.

Vowell stepped gingerly over the yellow tape and headed for the front door entrance to examine the victim. He was a white male lying on his side suffering from what looked like at least two gunshot wounds, one to the head and one to the upper body. Vowell had seen enough corpses in his time to know that this one had been dead for about an hour.

As partner Bobby Williams pulled up at the curb out front of the house, assistant coroner Grover Tuten appeared at Vowell's side.

"Never stood a chance."

Tuten eventually officially pronounced the victim dead at the scene at 11:40 P.M.

Investigator Vowell then kicked in the system which is supposed to cover all homicides. He called police forensic expert Bill Adams on his cell phone and then contacted his boss, Sgt. Wayne Pinkston.

"You better haul ass over here soon as possible. Have a first looksee at what we got," said Vowell.

Jimmy Vowell was by nature a cautious man and he was not about to make any foregone conclusions about the case at such an early stage.

At that moment he did not know if it had been an intruder who had come to the door and shot the victim or exactly what had occurred. But it was a homicide and that was all that mattered.

Vowell had to be open-minded at first. "You have to be in this job. I didn't want to have any kind of tunnel vision that would lead me to believe it was definitely an intruder or whatever," he later recalled.

Just then Vowell noticed a blue Cavalier parked around the back of the property. He quickly established that it belonged to the victim's wife, Gina Spann, who'd made the original 911 call.

Gina told one of the first deputies on the scene that she, her son and a friend had arrived from town, seen the body and called 911. Vowell then established that the occupants of the car had been Gina Spann, Larry Wayne Kelley and Spann's twelve-year-old son Michael.

Vowell moved into the back of the house and began speaking gently to Gina and the other two to try and establish the scenario.

He immediately noticed they were acting "kinda frantic." They told Vowell they'd come in through the back door and found Kevin Spann. Vowell wondered why they didn't come through the front door as they wouldn't have been able to see the victim from the street.

Also, instead of using the phone that was active in the house they went down to the corner store and called 911. Jimmy Vowell thought that was kind of strange, too.

He then suggested that fellow investigator Bobby Williams interview Kelley and Spann individually while he would continued examining the scene.

Crime-scene technician Bill Adams then arrived at the house and began the process of inspecting the area in minute detail. He slowly walked through the house with lead investigator Sgt. Wayne Pinkston carefully sketching the layout before photographing the scene of death.

After all the preliminaries had been completed, coroner Tuten released the victim to be taken to the University Hospital in Augusta.

Crime technician Adams then walked around the perimeter of the house to see if there were any signs of a forced entry. There was nothing to report to investigators Pinkston, Vowell and Williams except a suspicious lack of any clues that strangers had called at the house.

A few minutes later Vowell talked to neighbors to see if they had seen or heard anything. The second one he called on mentioned that the previous morning at approximately 12:30 A.M. someone had fired a shot through a window at 3805 Old Waynesboro. Vowell called in to his office and discovered from the previous night's police report that $200 had been taken from the victim's wallet and his 1986 Toyota Corolla had been stolen.

Meanwhile Bobby Williams was interviewing Larry Kelley in the back seat of his Pontiac Bonneville outside the Spann house. Williams was surprised when Kelley spoke about his relationship with Spann. He made it clear they were sleeping together at the house. It seemed a highly unconventional arrangement.

A few minutes later Jimmy Vowell read Bobby Williams' notes of what Larry Kelley had said, which made him even more suspicious.

At about 9:30 P.M. tonight me, Gina and Michael left the house and went to Blockbuster Video on Highway 23 to return some movies. We left there and went to Rallys Hamburgers on Highway 25 at Lumpkin Road. We left there at about 10:15 P.M. and went to my friend

Chris's house on Fernwood Circle and stayed there for a while and talked.

We left there at about 10:30 P.M. and started home. We stopped at the Crown Station at Highway 56 and Tobacco Road to get something to drink. We left there and came home. We pulled in the driveway beside the Mustang. Gina and Michael and I walked in the back door. Gina walked out of the den and into the living room. Then about a minute later ran back in the kitchen and told me and Michael to get out of the house.

We went out the back door and to the car. Gina came into the car and she was crying . . .

What most concerned Jimmy Vowell was that a teenage boy could be so specific about times and locations. It was almost as if he'd rehearsed what he was going to say.

Then his fellow investigator Bobby Williams talked with Gina Spann who wouldn't—or couldn't—explain why she was sleeping with a young guy in the same house as her husband and son. She made no claim that her husband was beating her.

During Gina Spann's unofficial first interview with Bobby Williams, she also gave virtually a minute-by-minute account of what she'd been doing that night. The detective knew from previous experience that most people were not so lucid just a few minutes after finding a husband shot to death.

When Bobby Williams recounted to Jimmy Vowell what Gina Spann and Larry Kelley had said, it once again struck them both that everything was too well rehearsed.

As Vowell later explained: "I didn't understand how they could be so clear about things after such a traumatic event. They said they'd been for a pizza, got a video and could even tell us the exact times they visited each place."

At the same time, just half a mile away, Deputy Marty Martinez was out on patrol when he came across Gina Spann's missing white four-door '86 Toyota Corolla.

He spotted the abandoned car illegally parked on the junction of Pearl Avenue and Browns Lane. A license check immediately confirmed that the vehicle was owned by Kevin Leroy Spann, of 3805 Old Waynesboro Road. After calling it in, Martinez was informed that the vehicle was connected to a homicide just committed over on Waynesboro Road.

Officer Martinez noted in his report that the steering column of the car was still intact. Both driver's and passenger's windows were left down. There was no radio inside the consul and a pair of black jeans were left in the rear seat with what appeared to be a set of keys in the middle consul. Also, all four doors to the vehicle were unsecured.

The only damage to the vehicle appeared to be on the front nearside bumper.

As Jimmy Vowell later recalled: "The clues were coming in fast and thick. The whole investigation seemed to be running itself."

Meanwhile Gina and Larry sat in the back of Bobby Williams's Pontiac while investigators Vowell and Williams decided what to do next. "We gonna finish up here and take them downtown and re-interview them and get to the bottom of what really happened here," Vowell told his partner.

Larry Kelley and Gina Spann were then separated and taken off in two black-and-silver RCSD cruisers with two deputies in each. Bobby Williams and Jimmy Vowell followed behind in their own vehicles.

As Vowell later said: "We'd already decided we would get pretty hard on them if we had to. The whole scenario stank. There was no way this guy had been killed by an intruder."

On arrival at 1 A.M. at the C.I.D. offices in downtown Augusta, Jimmy Vowell and his partner set themselves a challenge: to solve the Kevin Spann murder before the night was out.

They knew that this was the time to do it. If they waited until the morning the suspects might have sorted out their stories and had time to work things out. Jimmy Vowell had to hit them then.

They decided to fully interview Larry Kelley first because he was younger and they reckoned they'd get a whole lot more information from him.

"I hit him with a little random recall from his earlier statement to Bobby Williams," explained Vowell. "He started jumpin' around a bit. It didn't take long for the holes to begin appearing."

It took Vowell and Williams less than an hour before Larry Kelley admitted to them that Gina Spann had put the youths up to the killing for some insurance money. Kelley said she'd promised to pay them the money for carrying out the hit and he even confessed that they'd tried to kill Kevin Spann the previous night and shot through the window of the house while the victim was in the shower. They'd also stolen his car to make it look like a robbery attempt.

Kelley said that Gina Spann "got real uptight" about the boys not killing her husband that first night.

Jimmy Vowell was bemused by the machismo with which Larry Kelley confessed his role in the murder.

"It was like he was real proud of what he'd done. Once he figured we knew what had happened he said, 'Okay, I'll tell you all about it and who the other players were.' How dumb can you get?"

Meanwhile Gina Spann was kept in a separate room throughout her lover's interview. Both investigators knew that the longer they were with Kelley the more nervous she would become.

TWENTY-TWO

Larry Kelley's interview with detectives provided a fascinating insight into how the plan to kill Gina's husband had evolved. Kelley explained to the investigators: "We'd been thinking of ways of killing Kevin Spann for about a month. We, being Gina Spann and me. And then my friend Chris Bargeron found these two guys. Chris lives up there on Fernwood Circle with his mom Debra.

"Anyhow, these two guys Chris found staged the burglary on the Saturday night. Actually this thing was supposed to go down that Saturday night.

"We picked one of them up Saturday night and took him out to the house where he then stole the car. He didn't shoot out the window then. He went back later and got his friend and then they shot through the window. But they did steal the car first."

But Larry Kelley was most concerned about one separate aspect of the case.

"I gotta say here and now that little Mike had no idea what was happening. What I'm basically saying is that me and Gina conspired to have Kevin shot.

"I brought Chris Bargeron in on it and these two guys he found were promised fifteen thousand dollars by Gina. I guess it would have happened once the insurance money was paid.

"It's kinda weird because I'm not sure Gina even knew where to find those two guys to pay them their money. Even Chris, who recruited them, had only known them about a week. I don't even think Gina would know where they lived or their full names."

Then Kelley astounded the two investigators by claiming he couldn't even remember what the two teenage assassins looked like. "They were white but I don't know where they came from. Nothing. I don't even know their first names. I don't reckon Gina does either. I wasn't looking at them when we rode in the car together. I wouldn't know them if they walked in here now. Reckon that's the best way to be."

Larry Kelley also mentioned that Gina was pregnant by him. The investigators raised their eyebrows. It seemed that Gina Spann did not do things by halves.

Eventually the two investigators emerged from the interview room with Larry Kelley and instructed two deputies to take him down to one of the holding cells. Then they called Gina in.

"Now, Ms. Spann, we've already advised you of your Miranda rights, is that correct?"

"Yes."

"And you understand those rights, is that correct?"

"Yes."

"Okay, I'm going to read them to you again for the benefit of the tape and I want you to follow along with me on the waiver of counsel form, okay?"

"Yes."

"You have the right to remain silent. Do you understand that?"

"Yes."

"Anything you say can and will be used against you in a court of law. Do you understand that?"

"Yes."

"You have the right to talk to a lawyer and to have him present with you while you are being questioned, do you understand that?"

"Yes."

"If you cannot afford to hire a lawyer one will be appointed to represent you before any questioning if you wish. Do you understand that?"

"Yes."

"You can decide at any time to exercise these rights and not answer any questions or make any statements. Do you understand that?"

"Yes."

"Do you understand each of these rights that I've explained to you?"

"Yes."

"Having these rights in mind, do you want to talk to me now?"

"Yes."

Recalled Jimmy Vowell: "I gotta say that earlier outside the house and as we walked into the detective bureau she'd seemed full of piss and vinegar. But once we got her into the interview room and told her what Kelley had said, she didn't take long in tellin' us precisely where we could find these other guys."

Vowell was struck by how calm Gina Spann was about the whole thing. As he later recalled: "Guess it was because it all came down to money and you know how that can deaden the senses. She just used these guys to get rid of her old man. Apart from Larry they seemed to mean very little to her."

Gina Spann went through the entire lead-up to the crime. But she insisted the murder plan was provoked by her husband's ill treatment of her.

She said: "It wasn't like I just started talking about killing my husband. It came about because he raped me and I was pissed and I was hurt."

But she was vague about exactly when Kevin Spann "raped" her, as she'd claimed.

"It was right after Larry moved in, about a week or so after Larry moved in. As to the date, I don't know. Larry was at work one night, I got off from work earlier."

Then she insisted that Larry Kelley knew all about the alleged attack.

"He [Kevin] raped me. I said no and he did it anyway. And I said, 'God, I wish he was dead,' to Larry."

However, Gina insisted there had not been a long-term plan to kill her husband.

"I just said I wished he was dead. I was tired of living the way I had been living and I couldn't deal with it anymore."

Gina told investigators she never thought the murder-for-hire scheme would actually go ahead.

"I guess Larry and me started talking about it more. I don't know if you'd call it more seriously. I mean we talked about it but I don't think either of us ever thought it was going to happen."

She even told investigators how Larry Kelley's friend Chris Bargeron had met someone at a party who said he could find someone to kill her husband.

"Next thing I knew everybody knew. I don't know all their names. I'm talking about people that I don't know. I don't even know these people."

Gina told police she didn't know the last names of the youths she hired to kill her husband.

"There was somebody named Matt. Somebody named Gerry. I never heard any of their last names. I know, I know where one of them lives but I don't know anything more about them.

"I still don't know Matt and Gerry's last names. Matt's the short one, white, about seventeen with short brown hair. I don't know what color his eyes are. But I do know he's just had his appendix out. He said he had them out a week ago.

"Gerry's taller than Matt. I don't know how tall. Maybe as tall as Larry with short hair. I think he said he was eighteen. He lives at the Royal Palms Motel as well. Been there about two weeks."

She also told Vowell and Williams about Chris Bargeron.

"I think Chris lives behind the Corral. But I don't know the name of the place. There was also some guy called Randy up there at the motel when they were talking about it."

When confronted by investigators about the failed attempt the night before Kevin Spann died she admitted: "It's true I did take one guy out there to get the car on the Saturday night. They were supposed to kill him [Kevin] that night.

"But I didn't think they had any intention of doing it. You know, all that bullshit type thing. He [Horne] was trying to act big for his friends. I didn't think he was going to do it.

"I was relieved when they didn't page me to say they were done on the Saturday night. I went home and I was relieved and everything was fine.

"I didn't want to report the car stolen but I didn't have a choice. Kevin made me report the car stolen."

But she did admit she was the one who took the money out of Kevin Spann's wallet.

"I just wanted to go shopping. I wanted that bank card and the money. Simple as that."

By around 3 A.M. investigators had established that Gina Spann had conspired with four other individuals to have her husband, Kevin Leroy Spann, killed. The crime was for $300,000 life insurance on the victim of which $200,000 was through the U.S. Army at Fort Gordon where Spann worked.

Investigator Jimmy Vowell had been supposed to clock off his shift at 1:30 A.M. but he knew there was a realistic chance of wrapping up the entire case within hours of the murder being committed. "There was no way I'd walk away from that," he later said.

Just before Gina Spann's interview ended, Jimmy Vowell left the room.

There was the problem of what to do with 12-year-old Michael, who'd been kept in a side office throughout his mom's interrogation. Vowell made out a child abuse report in order to get him taken to a safe haven. He was given a bed for that night by one of the clerics at the Fort Gordon base after he was contacted by Augusta police.

Then Vowell went with lead investigator Sgt. Wayne Pinkston to the Royal Palms Motel where Spann had told them Piazzi and Horne were waiting for the others to show up.

Jimmy Vowell called for two black-and-silvers to escort them to the motel. They assigned two deputies to Spann and Kelley to await their return. The night was far from over.

TWENTY-THREE

At 4:30 A.M.—less than six hours after Kevin Spann's murder—Jimmy Vowell and Sgt. Wayne Pinkston stopped their vehicles two hundred yards from the Royal Palms Motel. Then they linked up with three deputies—Gerald Tanksley, Alan Alspaugh and Daniel Choate—in two RCSD cruisers.

Vowell believed the suspects could still be armed so he needed sufficient cover just in case the youths got trigger-happy.

The four police vehicles quietly moved up the street to the rear entrance of the motel. Guns drawn, the five officers then headed silently up one flight of stairs to room 20.

Jimmy Vowell knocked hard on the door before stepping aside in case shots were fired.

At first there was no response so Vowell rapped even harder with the butt of his gun.

A bleary-eyed Gerry Horne opened the door a few seconds later. He was in no fit state to put up a struggle and neither was his partner-in-crime Matt Piazzi.

Jimmy Vowell noticed that they seemed relieved to have been caught. Piazzi began sobbing. The deputies cuffed the two suspects and took them both down to separate patrol cars to wait for Vowell and Pinkston.

The two investigators then gave the room a thorough search because they wanted to wrap the whole investigation up by finding the murder weapon. Much to their disappointment there was no sign of it.

Vowell and Pinkston headed back down to talk to the boys who were each sitting in separate black-and-silvers. Vowell got in the back seat beside Piazzi, who was shaking like a leaf and immediately told him exactly what had happened.

Piazzi related to Vowell how after the shooting the two of them phoned for a radio cab from the Fast Fare store at the junction with Tobacco Road and Highway 56. He said they were taken to Ryan's Steakhouse and then walked to the Royal Palms Motel where Horne was registered.

Vowell asked about the murder weapon.

"You mean the .38?" asked Piazzi.

"A .38 what, inch belt?" Vowell asked, because he wanted Piazzi on the record talking about the specific weapon.

"A .38 pistol," came Piazzi's response.

"Yes, that's right."

"I can take you to it," said a very shaky Piazzi.

Jimmy Vowell knew that finding the murder weapon was paramount so he interrupted Piazzi and told him he would have to accompany them immediately to the location where he'd thrown the gun away.

Less than thirty minutes later, investigators with flashlights recovered the .38 under a bush behind Forward Augusta on the east side of Amoco Polymers.

Before the investigators returned to the RCSD C.I.D. offices in Augusta with their suspects, Horne gave Vowell a full address for Chris Bargeron, the youth they said had recruited them for the hit.

Vowell and Williams arrived shortly afterwards at 2079 Fernwood Circle and through the front window saw Chris Bargeron asleep on a couch in the living room. They knocked on the door and Bargeron opened it bleary-eyed. He didn't put up a struggle. Vowell then informed his mother Debra Bargeron that her son had been involved in a shooting and would have to go with them. Deputy Choate then transported Bargeron to the C.I.D. offices downtown.

Chris Bargeron proved to be much less forthcoming about the role he played in the death of Kevin Spann.

After being read his Miranda rights, Bargeron insisted that, following the first attempt on the previous night, he had thought he was no longer involved in the attempt to kill Spann.

As he began to explain his position to investigators, Bargeron stopped giving his statement and insisted that a lawyer be present before he continued. Investigators were left with no choice but to halt the interview immediately.

Bargeron was the only suspect who had not fully confessed to his role in the murder of Kevin Spann.

But then, Chris Bargeron was the only one of the four youths who had extensive previous experience of problems with the police. He knew that it would be foolish to say or do anything without a lawyer present.

*   *   *

Meanwhile Matt Piazzi was telling investigators that he did not know Chris Bargeron very well. He made it sound as though he had fallen into the role of hitman almost by accident.

He told police: "I don't even know Chris's last name. He's about five-eight, five-nine, heavy-set, black hair, a white male. I don't even remember the road where he lives. But it's close to the Royal Palms, about a block away. Hey, it's down Lumpkin Road, it was down Lumpkin Road."

But he had much better recall of the weapon used by them.

Piazzi proudly informed investigators: "It was a .38 snubnose special. Chrome with a black handle. I was under the impression the gun belonged to Gina."

Piazzi also told detectives that Horne had taken a pot shot at another house as the two youths traveled back from the failed hit on Saturday night.

He said the original plan for Saturday night was that Gerry Horne would go in the house and "shoot him, shoot the guy." He couldn't even remember Kevin Spann's name.

Piazzi claimed that Gina Spann had definitely mentioned a sum of fifteen thousand dollars. "We were goin' to split it three ways. Me, Chris and Jerry. She said the money was coming from an insurance policy on him."

The young man's description of what had happened was so calm and matter-of-fact that it led some of the investigators to surmise that he simply didn't realize the full seriousness of the crime he had committed.

Like Larry Kelley before him, Piazzi sounded extremely proud of what he'd done. As Jimmy Vowell later described it: "These kids just didn't get it. They'd murdered some guy in cold blood but they acted like it was some video game."

Piazzi continued. "So we all get in her car—a black convertible—and she takes us up to Covington. Jerry had the gun throughout all this. It was the same one we used the day before.

"Then we both start walking up towards the house and he [Horne] hands me the gun. I cocked it and knocked on the door and then shoot the guy twice. Once in the chest and I think once in the head. Then we pretty much haul ass."

Next thing Piazzi recalled was the police knocking on the door of room 20 at the Royal Palms Motel.

"And then they all come in and throw us down and handcuff us and take us, take me out to the road and then take me to the Augusta Sheriff's Department.

"It was not my sole intention to begin with to go out there and shoot this man for the fifteen thousand dollars but we did it all at the last minute. She wanted it done."

Then Piazzi added with a hint of pride: "I am giving this statement freely and voluntarily. Nobody's made any threats against me. I'm not under any duress."

Vowell and Williams had concluded the first stage of the investigation. In their report they wrote:

> On the previous morning of 5-11-97 at 12:30 A.M. Piazzi and Horne were dropped off near the family house on Waynesboro by Gina Spann

and her boyfriend Larry Wayne Kelley. They then walked to the residence and where Horne fired one shot into a bedroom window and the two took the victim's Toyota, which they were told to do by Gina Spann.

Later that same day at approximately 10:46 P.M. on 5-11-97, after having been dropped off near the same location by Gina Spann and Larry Kelley, Horne and Piazzi proceeded to the residence at which time the victim answered the front door and was shot once in the left cheek just below his eye by Piazzi who was armed with a nickel plated five shot Taurus revolver (serial number filed away). The victim possibly was shot in the upper chest area but it will not be determined until after the autopsy is performed.

At the time of the shootings, Gina Spann, Larry Kelley and Spann's 12–year-old son Michael were away from the residence since it had been predetermined that they be away when Kevin was to be killed.

In plain detective terms, Gina Lynn Spann had conspired with her boyfriend, Larry Wayne Kelley, to hire someone to kill her husband for her. Kelley got his friend, 16-year-old Christopher Lee Bargeron of 2079 Fernwood Circle to get in touch with Gerald Lewis Horne, 18, and his friend, 16-year-old Matthew Clark Piazzi to kill Mr. Spann. Bargeron, Piazzi and Horne were each to get $5,000.00 for killing Mr Spann.

At 5 A.M. mugshots of the suspects were taken by Jimmy Vowell. All five were completely expressionless, except for Chris Bargeron who had a slight smirk on his face. He knew he'd be the difficult one to pin the crime on because he had not signed a statement like the others.

Kelley, Horne, Bargeron and Piazzi were all taken to Richmond County Youth Detention Center after giving their statements. Gina Spann went to the county lock-up just outside Augusta.

Investigator Jimmy Vowell couldn't quite believe he'd managed to wrap up an entire murder inquiry within seven hours of the crime being committed.

He recalled: "We actually got everyone in jail by the time Bobby Williams was due off the night turn at 6 A.M. that morning. The case seemed pretty airtight. I went home and went to bed. Not bad going for what had seemed like a random homicide just a few hours earlier."

Just after the two investigators clocked off duty, one of the deputies brought Matt Piazzi down to the processing room to be fingerprinted. The suspect asked the deputy what he was being charged with. He replied that he didn't know because he hadn't seen the paperwork on the case.

Piazzi then said, "Hell, I guess it's murder. I pulled the gun and shot the motherfucker."

TWENTY-FOUR

Investigator Jimmy Vowell had wrapped up a cold-blooded murder in record time but he was extremely concerned about one other aspect of the case.

Gerry Horne had clearly stated that Matt Piazzi claimed to have murdered someone else when he lived with his family in North Carolina.

So the following morning—May 12, 1997—Jimmy Vowell spoke to Horne again in room B-254 at the C.I.D. offices. Horne said that Piazzi had told him he had earlier killed his girlfriend's father by shooting him and that was why he wasn't worried about being the shooter in the Spann killing.

Horne said that on arriving back at the motel room after Piazzi had shot and killed Kevin Spann, Piazzi told him he'd committed the other murder because the father had raped his daughter.

According to Horne, Piazzi "said he'd shot the guy once in the chest and after he'd fallen he shot him twice more in the face with a .45 Colt he owned."

Horne then told detectives that Piazzi also said that his victim lived in an isolated area at least two miles from the nearest neighbors when the Piazzi family had lived in North Carolina.

Gerry Horne insisted to Jimmy Vowell that he played no part in this other murder, if it had even occurred.

But Horne said he thought Piazzi was serious about this other killing. "As serious as he was about what happened last night," he told Vowell. "I tell you he was real cold and unemotional when I saw him shoot Spann. It was kinda freaky."

Vowell then phoned Captain Steve Houck of the Ashe County, North Carolina, Sheriff's Department. He asked Houck if he knew of any unsolved murders that might fit the one Horne spoke about. Houck answered that he had been very familiar with Matthew Piazzi and his family when they lived in the county but that Piazzi had never been involved in anything as serious.

Houck said he'd ask around adjoining counties to see if anyone knew of a homicide that was unsolved and would call Vowell back. He also said he'd fax Vowell records he had on Piazzi.

A few minutes later Jimmy Vowell got a call from a reporter named Shannah Holden on *Hard Copy*, the tabloid TV show. She wanted to know some details on the case. She also wanted to come to Augusta to interview the investigators and also the defendants. The Kevin Spann slaying was turning into national news.

Vowell told Holden that he'd contact his boss, Deputy Chief Strength, which he did. He then called her back a short while later and said that Strength had advised him that he could handle the interview but *Hard Copy* could not at this stage go in to interview the defendants in jail.

Then Vowell got a call at about 11:50 A.M. from Gerry Horne's mother Mrs. Mabel Beatrice Horne. She wanted to know about upcoming court dates. Vowell told her there were none yet scheduled. She left Vowell her phone number in case he needed her for anything. He thanked her for that.

By mid-morning on Monday, May 12, Gina Spann, Piazzi, Kelley and Horne had all begun to realize that they should not give anything more away without a lawyer present. But as Jimmy Vowell later explained: "They'd confessed to everything so there wasn't a lot of point in worryin' 'bout things by that stage."

But there were a number of other individuals who seemed concerned about whether they might be implicated in the murder of Kevin Spann.

The morning after the killing, Larry Kelley's brother Michael came to the C.I.D. office and asked Jimmy Vowell for the paperwork on the case against Larry. Vowell told him he could only have an incident report.

It was clear that Michael Kelley was worried that the suspects might have alleged he was in some way involved in the crime.

Michael Kelley told Jimmy Vowell that about three weeks earlier, his mother, Carol Best, had seen a blue Chevrolet Cavalier with a white top near their home at 2720 Margaret Court. Later they discovered that the house had been burglarized.

Vowell surmised that the murder weapon must have been stolen during the burglary because he immediately recognized the description of the car as being similar to the one owned by Gina Spann.

Vowell then contacted Michael Kelley's stepfather, David Best, who said that in the burglary, there had been jewelry and a camera and some currency taken.

"What about a nickel-plated Taurus .38 pistol being taken?" asked Vowell.

"I don't think so. All my guns are locked up in my vault."

Vowell then asked Mr. Best to check the vault. He called Vowell back five minutes later and said he was in fact missing a pistol and he described it as being a .38 caliber nickel-plated Taurus with a 3-inch barrel and black Pachmeye grips. It had been loaded with five blue-tip ball-type ammunition.

It sounded identical to the weapon recovered in the field after Kevin Spann's murder. The ammunition also matched the description of what had been recovered.

Mr. Best told Vowell he got the gun when he traded a pistol with a man about four or five years earlier. He told Vowell that the man had said he'd purchased the pistol about eight or nine years ago from a local store called The Gun Cabinet. He also said that the man said he couldn't locate a serial number for the weapon.

Vowell then phoned The Gun Cabinet and was told that without a date of purchase it would be very difficult to locate the paperwork on the sale.

But he already knew he had the right weapon.

Vowell then spoke with investigator Greg Newsome who had been assigned to the burglary at the Best household. He told Newsome that Larry Kelley was the perpetrator of the burglary. It seemed a safe assumption since the blue Cavalier seen by his mother, Carol Best, matched the one driven by Gina Spann. He also asked Larry Kelley's stepfather to drive his wife out to the Spann house on Old Waynesboro Rd to look at the Cavalier parked out front and call him back with a tag number if it was the same vehicle.

TWENTY-FIVE

The day after Kevin Spann's murder, Richmond County's Deputy Chief Ronald Strength gave a press conference to explain what he believed was the motive behind the killing.

"It was two life-insurance policies on Mr. Spann's life, totaling $300,000 that Mrs. Spann was the beneficiary of. She had no job and nor did Mr. Kelley, although he is still currently a Butler High School eleventh-grader."

Strength admitted he and investigators did not yet know how long Gina Spann and Larry Kelley had been plotting to kill Kevin Spann.

"But it seems that the idea to kill Mr. Spann was his wife's. Once that decision was made, Mr. Kelley called his friend Mr. Bargeron, a Butler ninth-grader who then referred them to Mr. Piazzi and Mr. Horne. They were both offered $5,000 to be paid when the insurance-policy money was received."

Strength added dryly: "Mrs. Spann had time to change her mind. I gotta say that on both nights, Mrs. Spann and Mr. Kelley took her twelve-year-old son and went out while they waited for the killing to take place.

"Within a short time of the crime being committed we questioned both Mrs. Spann and Mr. Kelley separately and found that there were many inconsistencies in their statements. Those interrogations also led us to Mr. Piazzi, Mr. Horne and Mr. Bargeron."

Then Deputy Chief Strength made a sad public admission to the assembled journalists:

"You know, no crime juveniles commit surprises me anymore because they have access to weapons and will use them."

He ended the press conference by saying:

"All these youths are now being held without bond at the Youth Detention Center. Good day, ladies and gentlemen."

As one local reporter said at the time: "It was just about the most clear-cut murder case I'd ever come across in Augusta."

At Augusta's University Hospital Department of Pathology, coroner Dr. Stephen Mullins was assigned the task of performing the autopsy on Kevin Spann.

He found that the first bullet entered just below the right eye and then traveled through the sinuses to the back of the head.

On close examination investigators had found fragments of that bullet along the path in front of the Spanns' house.

Dr. Mullins concluded that this first wound was fatal and caused all systems to shut down within moments. In other words, Matt Piazzi's second shot wasn't even necessary.

The second bullet entered in the neck, to the right of the middle. It passed through the trachea, thyroid gland, possibly nicked the right carotid artery and then went on to the right upper lobe of the lung.

A distinct blue pellet was found in the left side posterior region of the victim.

Dr. Mullins also reported finding more fragments of this blue pellet and part of a copper bullet jacket was recovered from the body and turned over to police forensic investigator Bill Adams, who was present at the autopsy.

The results of the medical examination were vital for the pending legal case, but since all the suspects were already incarcerated the autopsy was able to be fairly straightforward.

Investigating crime-scene technician Adams reported back to C.I.D. that the victim had actually died of cerebral trauma which was secondary to the bullet wound.

Adams carefully placed several pieces of metal from the body along with two blue plastic bearings in plastic containers marked for later examination.

Then Bill Adams headed over to the car pound to carry out an examination of Gina Spann's white Toyota. He quickly located fingerprints that could be matched up to the suspects.

Investigators still had to locate the paperwork on the two insurance policies out on Kevin Spann's life. One was worth $100,000 and the other military policy worth $200,000.

On Tuesday, May 13, *The Augusta Chronicle* headlined the story of the alleged killers' arrest:

FIVE HELD IN SLAYING
Police say teens killed Fort Gordon soldier in
insurance-money plot of wife, live-in
boyfriend

After botching the first attempt Saturday
night, two teens went back to a Fort Gordon
soldier's house on Mother's Day, shot him in
the face and chest and killed him in a plot de-
vised by the soldier's 31-year-old wife and her
live-in teenage boyfriend, police said.

Kevin Leroy Spann, 35, a supervisor in Company D Signal Battalion 442 at Fort Gordon,
was pronounced dead at 11:40 P.M. at his home
at 3805 Old Waynesboro Road of gunshot
wounds, said Richmond County Deputy Coroner Grover Tuten.

The newspaper went on to tell its readers that
Hephzibah High School ninth-grade drop-out Matt
Piazzi had been charged with shooting Kevin Spann.

Gina Spann and Larry Wayne Kelley along with
Gerry Horn, and Chris Bargeron, were each charged
initially with being a party to the crime of murder.

Kelley was said by the newspaper to be a Butler
High School eleventh-grader. Horne was referred to
as a tenth-grader at Hephzibah High and Bargeron as
a Butler ninth-grader.

The paper highlighted one of the most disturbing
side issues of the case, that Gina had taken her 12-
year-old son with her when the killings were committed.

The report also informed readers that all the teen-agers were being held at the county Youth Detention Center.

The following day *The Augusta Chronicle* reported that all five suspects in the murder of Kevin Spann were to be charged with murder.

District Attorney Danny Craig told reporters that the charge of party to a crime had been changed to murder which meant that all the suspects would eventually be dealt with in a Superior Court.

It was clear that the authorities intended to throw the book at Gina Spann and her co-conspirators.

Two days after Kevin's murder Jason Swallow—Taco Bell worker and former tenant at the house on Old Waynesboro Road—called up the sheriff's department to find out about getting the remainder of his belongings out of the property.

Investigators immediately asked Swallow to go in for an interview at the C.I.D. offices. They wanted to know about the time Gina had asked to borrow his gun.

Swallow told them he'd purchased the semi-automatic .25 from another Taco Bell worker. He said Gina never mentioned what she wanted the gun for. And he also recalled how she never said anything again about the gun after that.

On that same day, Taco Bell worker Amanda Quick bumped into Larry Kelley's brother Michael on the Peach Orchard strip.

When Kelley told Amanda what had happened she was stunned. She couldn't believe they'd actually done something so serious.

Over at Taco Bell, the relatively harmless soap opera of Larry and Gina's romance had turned into a cold-blooded murder case. Everyone was talking about what had happened. "They said Gina had messed up them kids' heads and given 'em drugs and told them how they were goin' to live happily ever after with all that insurance money," recalled Amanda Quick.

"I reckon she probably did mess with their heads big time. Gina never really fitted in. I knew she was trouble the moment I laid eyes on her."

But for the bored kids of Taco Bell the real-life treachery of their former co-workers did provide some of them with a chance to enjoy their own "fifteen minutes of fame."

Two days after the killing a reporter from TV's *Hard Copy* showed up at Taco Bell on the Peach Orchard strip. Amanda Quick soon established herself as a star of that particular show.

"Hey, did you see me on *Hard Copy*?" she asked anyone who would listen.

She later told this author: "*Hard Copy* was real cool. Everyone saw me and phoned up to say how good I looked on it. This real neat reporter lady came up to our trailer. There was a camera guy, another with a microphone thing he put up my jersey. That was kinda weird. Hey, we got a copy of it on video someplace. You wanna see it?"

Amanda Quick breathlessly informed *Hard Copy* viewers that she saw Gina giving all those youths drugs at the motel. "I also told them she didn't carry herself too well," Amanda proudly recalled. "In many ways Gina looked older than she was. I always reckoned she was zoned out in her own little world. Then it all came crashin' down."

Two days after the murder, Larry Kelley's brother Michael admitted to investigators that Gina Spann had approached him and asked him if he would help her "take out" her husband.

Kelley told detectives: "I took her to mean to kill her husband. You know, and I ain't, I'm not going to take nobody's life for any reason. I told her no and that was the last time she ever brought it up."

Larry Kelley's brother then went public about his friendship with Gina Spann in *The Augusta Chronicle*. He reiterated what he'd told the police.

"I told her, you know, I told her flat out, 'I ain't doing it,'" he told the paper.

Kelley went on: "She was real sneaky about it. She was just like, you know, she asked me: 'Well, why won't you do it?'

"Or sometimes she'd say: 'This'll make your brother real happy.'"

But Kelley says he told her: "I ain't going to jail for nothing like that."

He told the *Chronicle*: "Any case I guessed my brother was already happy. No, sir, we never got into details. I didn't, really, I didn't want no part of it. That's what I told her the last time I said no."

He added: "I think my brother deserves to do some prison time for his role so he can learn a lesson . . . He's young. I hope he will get out and have time to live a good life and do things right. They were all old enough to know better, but they were still kids . . . very impressionable."

Michael Kelley was convinced that his kid brother and the other youths were on drugs when they committed the murder, although subsequent police tests completely ruled this out.

"I think she just kept getting them high until they were in the right state of mind. If you're high, you get the feeling that you can't get caught and you feel invincible."

Then Michael Kelley piled on the pressure for Gina Spann to face the death penalty.

"I think she deserves the electric chair. She messed up five lives—including her own son because now he doesn't have a mother or a father."

As news of the murder of Kevin Spann spread throughout Georgia, Joe Harrod became so worried that he might be implicated in the murder that he called up lead investigator Wayne Pinkston at Augusta C.I.D.

He told Pinkston he thought that others might be throwing out his name as being involved in the Spann hit.

Harrod told the officer that he used to work with Gina and Larry and said that about two months earlier they had approached him and asked him to kill Kevin for them. She claimed Kevin had beaten and raped her in the past. He said that Gina also told him that she wanted him killed for insurance monies.

Then there was the problem of what to do with Gina Spann's white Toyota once it had been examined. Hundreds of dollars in collection charges were due.

When Bobby Williams spoke to Gina Spann in jail

she didn't have anyone to pick up the car except Larry Kelley's brother Michael.

At 9:30 A.M. on May 14—less than three days after Kevin Spann's murder—Gina's sister Jody Pierce visited her at the Richmond County Jail.

Gina had an ulterior motive for wanting to see her estranged sister, who had specially traveled down from Illinois.

After a token greeting, Gina told Jody that when her Cavalier was searched by police after the killing they didn't find the insurance papers that were relevant to the case.

Kevin Spann's policies and his will plus relevant paperwork had all been put together and hidden in the car trunk by Gina before the murder was committed.

She told her sister that the paperwork was under a piece of cardboard in the rear compartment. Gina then specially signed papers in the jail to get her car keys released to her sister.

Jody—who was particularly outraged by her sister's treatment of Michael—immediately informed the Augusta police, who recovered all the policies.

And while being interviewed by grateful Augusta C.I.D. investigators, Jody Pierce also mentioned that Gina had told her she'd been talking to some other people in jail with her and she'd decided she was going to plead temporary insanity.

Her grounds were that she'd been put on new medication by her doctor after she'd told him how much she dreaded Mother's Day each year because of the death of her daughter Heather eleven years previously.

Jody told investigators that her sister had gotten the medical grounds idea from a notorious prisoner named Ruth Vaiden—whom Jimmy Vowell had helped bring to justice after she murdered her own mother. Vaiden had been teaching Gina how to show that she was under mental stress at the time of her husband's murder.

Police interviewing Jody Pierce also wanted to know more about Gina's alleged pregnancy, which Larry Kelley had told them about.

The police had been so concerned by the possibility of a pregnancy that Deputy Chief Ron Strength had advised his investigators to establish the truth as quickly as possible because it could seriously affect the coming trials of the suspects.

Jody told investigators there was no chance her sister was pregnant. She later recalled: "It was Gina's way to keep a man. I couldn't believe she'd pulled the same trick with Kelley as she did with all those other guys."

Jody was so outraged she even told investigators that her sister's sterilization operation had been carried out in Fairview, Illinois, eleven years earlier.

"It was typical of Gina and there was no way I'd help her get off a murder charge," Jody later recalled.

A couple of days later, on May 16, 1997, Investigator Jimmy Vowell was sent a videotape of Gina Spann by Jody Pierce.

Vowell viewed part of the tape and heard a voice referring to shooting someone. The tape also included shots of Gina and her young lover Jesse Dunn having

sexual intercourse. Jody even warned Vowell that her
sister was "a raunchy person."

In a note she included in the package to Investigator Vowell, she wrote:

> Like I told you, you probably don't want to
> go any further than that part. If you do you'll
> be seeing things you really don't want to. Just
> a little warning. If you need anything let me
> know.
> Thanks,
> Jody Pierce

A few days after the murder of Kevin Spann, Shanna
Quick had a chilling phone conversation with one of
the youths who'd bragged about his involvement with
Piazzi and Horne on the Saturday night just before
the attempt on Kevin which ended in a bullet hole in
Michael's bedroom window.

"Did you know they planned to kill the guy?" she
asked this particular youth.

"Yeah. I was goin' to go down there with them."

"You tellin' me you were going to go down there
and do that?"

The youth hesitated.

"Well, not exactly. No, I wasn't goin' to do it myself."

To this day, Shanna doesn't even know if the police realized that this youth was involved.

The Spann murder case shocked thousands of servicemen and -women based at Fort Gordon. But it
wasn't the first time a Fort Gordon soldier had been

the victim of a murder-for-insurance-money plot.

Twenty-five years earlier Fort Gordon Private Kenneth Barnes, 19, from Ohio, was shot to death by men hired by his wife who was only finally arrested more than ten years later.

Elsewhere in the nation in May 1997 other crimes were catching people's attention.

In South Bend, Indiana, four white men were charged with killing a black man simply for revenge in an outrageous racially motivated murder case.

In Denver, the infamous Timothy McVeigh was being branded a terrorist in front of a federal jury following his arrest in connection with the Oklahoma City bombing outrage in 1995.

In Washington, the Justice Department asked for the death penalty to be imposed on Unabomber suspect Theodore Kaczynski.

Back in Augusta, a man was charged with cruelty to children after the death of his teenage son.

The brutal murder of Kevin Spann was, tragically, just another statistic in the bloody history of American homicides.

TWENTY-SIX

At the time of Kevin Spann's murder, Matt Piazzi's father, Richard, had thought his son had stopped hanging around with Gerry Horne and a number of other people he considered as troublemakers.

So Mr. Piazzi was bewildered by the police accusations against his son, the so-called triggerman in a hitman-style execution.

Like many parents who discover another side to their children, Richard Piazzi at first refused to believe his son was even involved.

He told one newsman who turned up at the family's modest house just a mile from where Kevin Spann was shot to death: "I don't know exactly what happened yet. But I would hate to think he did something like that. I can't believe my son did this. Something went wrong. I don't know what happened yet, but it didn't sound right that all of those boys would be hanging around that woman."

As one of the investigators commented after hearing the remarks, "How many times have I heard a mom or dad say that about their child?"

Not surprisingly, many of Kevin Spann's co-workers at Fort Gordon were having a tough time coming to terms with his death. Army chaplains at the base worked extensively with many of his colleagues who were shocked by the news.

Since the murder, Gina's son Michael had been staying with one of the Fort Gordon chaplains while arrangements were being made with the Pierce family for him to be picked up and taken to Gina's sister's home in Illinois.

A memorial service for Kevin Spann was held at 10 A.M. on Wednesday, May 14. It was a strictly soldiers-only event.

Kevin's commanding officer Lt. Col. Steven Maida, commander of 442 Signal Battalion, told the service: "Kevin Spann was a well-liked and professional soldier. His loss is regretted by all who worked and served with him."

The service, at Barnes Avenue Chapel inside Fort Gordon, was marked by a horn playing *Taps*. All of the soldiers' names from the 442 Signal Battalion were called out and they answered "present"—but when Staff Sgt. Kevin Leroy Spann's name was read, the only thing heard were sobs from 12-year-old Michael.

Kevin Spann's co-workers, supervisors and clergy tried to comfort the boy, attempting to come up with words that might help him deal with the killing of the man whom he considered his father.

Fort Gordon Chaplain Williams told the 100 soldiers who came to pay their last respects: "I can't begin to experience the loss you are experiencing . . . Sometimes God allows us to ask the questions, like: 'Why? How?' . . . Sometimes it just doesn't make sense.

"What shall we say in response to this [death]?" Chaplain Williams continued. He told Michael to think of St. Paul, who said: " 'The absolute greatest gift is the gift of forgiveness.' "

Robin Eoute, who was trained by Kevin Spann to train other soldiers, delivered the eulogy. She said he'd taught her how to solve problems without worrying about them.

"He motivated me whenever I had a problem. He would make a joke and solve it like it wasn't a problem at all," she told the service.

Company Commander Felix Castro, one of Kevin Spann's immediate supervisors, said the staff sergeant was an outstanding leader and technically proficient and knowledgeable.

He trained lieutenants who were going to be signal officers in the Army. He had worked most of his career in communications.

It was even revealed that Kevin Spann would have graduated that very day and become eligible to be an Army recruiter. He was also going to be permanently transferred to South Carolina.

Most of Kevin Spann's colleagues had no idea what was going on in his personal life.

"He talked about his son, Michael, all the time. When we were at an Easter event, they hugged a lot and it was nice to see that," said Cmmdr. Castro.

At the funeral Kevin Spann's father, Harold, was as bewildered as everyone else by the death of his beloved son.

He had been aware of the family's unusual living arrangements at the house on Old Waynesboro Road but Harold Spann believed that his son's only aim was to make sure Michael was being properly brought up.

"I was very proud of Kevin. He was so happy to be in the military," he told Kevin's commanding officer.

A couple of days after Gina Spann's arrest her ex-lover Jesse Dunn got a strange phone call from a woman claiming to be one of Gina's friends.

Jesse was extremely worried by the tone of the phone call.

"It was somebody who'd been in Gina's cell. They tracked me down. I didn't like it because I never wanted to hear from Gina Spann again. I thought she was a psycho," he later recalled.

The caller told Jesse Dunn that Gina wanted him to know what had happened and that she was in jail. The woman's name was Vivian Harrison and Gina had convinced her that her husband had brutalized her and provoked his own murder.

Jesse Dunn was alarmed to discover Harrison had called his parents' house first because that was the only phone number she had. Dunn heard from his parents that the caller had made up a story about a friend of Jesse's being in the hospital so as to ensure he would get the message and call back.

Dunn called the number back. He knew it had to be Gina.

"I was thinking it was Gina, you know, playing her games because she always lied like that and I called and it was some lady saying that she was her cellmate and that she was in, in the detention center and that she didn't know if I wanted to know where she was, at but you know, that's where she was," Jesse Dunn later recalled.

"She didn't say why she'd called. All she said was Gina did not know whether you wanted to know where she was at or not."

According to Jesse Dunn the actual conversation was bizarre, to say the least:

> "Gina's in jail."
> "So? It's no surprise," replied Jesse Dunn.
> When he heard what she was in jail for he was even more unsurprised.
> "The stupid bitch finally got the guts to do whatever she was going to do, huh?"

As Jesse Dunn later explained: "I didn't even know what had happened to Kevin until that cellmate person called me. As soon as I heard that, okay, I told a few people that are on the net and they instantly called me the next day and were like, 'You need to check out this www.augustachronicle.com.'

"So I looked at it and I was just dumfounded. I was like, 'Wow, that's crazy, because that house was like in the picture and I like lived there.'"

Later Jesse Dunn admitted: "I was kinda relieved when the police called me up. I'd been trying to stay out of that particular hole. I was hopin' I wouldn't get involved. But I realized I'd have to talk to them some time. I thought they were goin' to subpoena me or some kind of shit.

"Personally, I hope they get her, give her what she deserves because she can't get away with that. I'd like the police to keep me informed because now that I'm officially involved I might as well know what's happening."

Settled back in Wieron, West Virginia, Jesse had gotten himself a full-time job working at a computer company and was trying to rebuild his life after Gina had almost destroyed it.

Meanwhile Augusta police confirmed that the latest official charges facing Gina and her four co-conspirators were malice murder, felony murder and possession of a firearm during the commission of certain crimes.

The prosecution of the five suspects was being managed by energetic Augusta District Attorney Danny Craig.

Craig had been district attorney and chief prosecutor for the Augusta Judicial Circuit since 1993. The 43-year-old DA practiced civil, criminal and domestic law in Augusta for fourteen years before winning office.

Craig was recognized as a hard-nosed DA determined to win prosecutions at any reasonable price. Craig had his fair share of critics amongst the city's legal fraternity but no one could deny his successes as DA.

Some found his slightly abrasive style difficult to deal with, while others—especially the local police— were full of admiration for his efforts to prosecute their hard-fought cases.

Away from the courts, Danny Craig served as secretary of the Prosecuting Attorney's Council of Georgia as well as teaching at the state's law enforcement academy and the national school for prosecutors in Columbia.

Danny Craig and his prosecution team originally scheduled the trials of Gina Spann and her four co-defendents for as early as possible but there were several issues that still had to be resolved before they could go ahead.

Because the U.S. Supreme Court had prohibited the execution of people under the age of 17, Craig quickly decided not to seek the death penalty against the two 16-year-olds charged in the case, Chris Bargeron and Matt Piazzi, even though Piazzi had been the triggerman.

Craig refused to make up his mind about whether to seek the death penalty against Larry Kelley should he be convicted of murder. Significantly, Craig was not seeking it against Gerry Horne.

But in the case of Gina Spann, Craig made his feelings known loud and clear: "The formal notice of intention to seek the death penalty in Ms. Spann's case alleges aggravating circumstances—that she directed another to commit murder. In layman's terms, that's a murder for hire," he explained just a few days after Gina Spann's arrest.

But there were other forces at work that would probably tip the balance in favor of a custodial sentence for Gina Spann despite the DA's threats.

Women were rarely subjected to capital murder trials in Georgia. According to the State Department of Corrections, only four women had been sentenced to death, and each was re-sentenced to life in prison. Three Augusta lawyers with capital murder trial experience had already publicly said that they couldn't think of a prosecutor ever seeking the death penalty against a woman in the Augusta Judicial Circuit since at least 1976, when the death penalty was reinstated.

The closest such case in the Augusta Judicial Circuit was in Lincoln County when Emma R. Cunningham was sentenced to death in October 1979. She was re-sentenced to life in prison in October 1982 and paroled in November 1990.

DA Danny Craig had another alleged murder-for-hire killing in the Augusta Judicial Circuit, but he refused to comment about the possibility of seeking the death penalty against the spouse in that case. Now with Gina Spann he had a second high-profile female killer on his hands. As one legal observer in the city pointed out at the time: "Danny Craig wants to make one of these women an example and he'll get there in the end. He's that kind of guy."

Just days after the Spann killing, investigators in neighboring Burke County charged Kenneth Alan Anderson, 27, with murder. Mr. Anderson was accused of hiring Charles DeWayne Reeves, 20, and Bernard Edward Meadows, 19, to kill his wife Kristia Anderson in order to collect life insurance. Ms. Anderson was found shot to death May 4 in her car. Because those involved were men there was no doubt in Danny Craig's mind that he could pursue the death penalty for that case.

Danny Craig's assistant DA, Nancy B. Johnson, handled much of the background research into the Kevin Spann murder case and she was the first prosecutor to view the video that Richmond County detectives had been given by Gina's sister Jody. It showed Gina having sex with Jesse Dunn and then openly bragging about shooting her husband.

Nancy Johnson later explained that until she watched the videotape she had not even been sure of Gina Spann's guilt. "But that completely swung it for me. That woman intended to kill her husband—there was no doubt about it. It was such a bizarre, stupid thing to do to make that tape," Johnson later recalled.

But this wasn't the only video which provided prosecutors with some invaluable evidence. Just a short distance from the house on Waynesboro Road, an off-duty cop had been videotaping a big catch of fish he'd made earlier that day when he heard the gunshots that ended Kevin Spann's life. The time code on the video would prove to be crucial evidence for establishing when the killing occurred.

Prosecutors eventually ended up with both videos on the same tape for court evidence purposes. As Nancy Johnson described it: "It seemed kinda bizarre when we played it back and there was a bunch of dead fish smoking in some cop's back yard."

In some ways those fish summed up the predicament of Gina Spann and her teenage accomplices.

Gina Spann's own court-appointed lawyer was Maureen Floyd, who said she took the case because she truly believed Gina was innocent.

Maureen Floyd was raised in a small town in South Carolina. Her father was a psychiatric social worker and her mother a nurse. She claimed she witnessed so much injustice during her youth that it inspired her to go to Washington DC to work for then-President Carter's re-election campaign.

As she explained: "In my younger days I was struck by the importance of fighting for the causes you believe in and Carter seemed the most genuine politician I'd ever come across."

In 1981 Maureen Floyd went to law school in South Carolina and decided to concentrate on criminal law. Since the mid-80s she had handled eight homicide trials.

Floyd immediately advised Gina Spann not to talk anymore to investigators. She knew that defending a woman who'd already made a confession would be a very difficult task, but she was determined to give it her best shot.

On Saturday, May 24, *The Augusta Chronicle* under headlines reading, "3 TEENS ACCUSE WOMAN— Youths say slain soldier's wife tried to entice them to murder her husband," reported that three more teenagers had told police that Gina had asked them to kill Kevin Spann.

First to talk about his peripheral involvement had been Larry Kelley's brother Michael. The other two were not named but it later emerged that they were Jesse Dunn and Jason Swallow.

Chief Deputy Ronald Strength insisted to newsmen: "We have no reason to believe that those statements we received from them are inaccurate."

In the same article, Taco Bell worker Amanda Quick told how Gerry Horne was playing with a gun when she visited his room on the Friday before the killing. Any doubters in Augusta were rapidly concluding that Gina and her young co-defendants were guilty as charged.

TWENTY-SEVEN

The four teenagers accused of killing Kevin Spann were by this time facing the stark reality of their situation inside Richmond County Youth Detention Center. There was virtually no exercise, no stereo, little television, few books, and even fewer visitors to break the monotony. Horne, Piazzi, Bargeron and Kelley's days in jail were interrupted only by occasional small chores. Except for a few days during which they were given psychological evaluations at a local hospital, their time was spent waiting for their next court appearance.

None of them were allowed to talk to each other in case they spoke about Kevin Spann's murder and how it happened. Bargeron was notably reluctant to even refer to the crime when it was mentioned by others he was incarcerated with.

Outside of visits from their families, an occasional friend and the attorneys representing them, the boys were locked up for more than twenty out of twenty-four hours of each day.

With the exception of Bargeron, none of the boys had any chance of being found innocent of murder because they'd all given statements to police. Their convictions were considered a near-certainty. It was just a question of how long their sentences would be—or so prosecutors hoped.

However, there was one person who vigorously questioned the guilt of Larry Kelley.

His attorney Mike Garrett believed that Larry only "went along for the ride" and should not have been facing murder charges as he was not directly involved in the murder of Kevin Spann.

But then, Mike Garrett was the type of man who would play every card he held in an effort to defend a client he felt had been unjustly accused of a crime.

In a recent appeal following the trial of a 15-year-old boy accused of murdering his best friend, Garrett had insisted the teenager thought the murder weapon had two empty chambers and he could pull the trigger twice without firing. Garrett told the appeals court judges that his client often played a game called "dry firing" in which he pointed the gun and pulled the trigger twice. His tragic victim was a willing participant in the so-called game. "He had no intention to discharge the pistol," argued Mike Garrett. His argument on that day in court just about summed up the steely determination of the man who was about to defend Gina Spann's teenage lover.

Garrett was a partner in the law firm Garrett and Gilliard, with offices in the Suntrust Bank Building at 801 Broad Street in downtown Augusta. Born on September 18, 1946, in Atlanta, he attended the Marist School before getting an A.B. with honors in 1968 at the University of North Carolina followed by a J.D. in 1973 from the University of Georgia. In a recent

Augusta Chronicle survey of lawyers in the area he was voted the one they would be most likely to choose if any of them were charged with a crime. As he says, "Guess I must be doin' something right."

Garrett did most of his criminal work in the Superior Courts of Richmond, Burke and Columbia Counties and in the Federal Courts in Georgia, South Carolina and Louisiana. He had a perfect record in death-penalty cases, which meant that none of his clients had ever been sentenced to die. Part of his success in this field could be attributed to his opposition to the death penalty.

Garrett explained: "The death penalty is a personal thing with me. I do not see how it serves any purpose in our society except vengeance. This purpose I see as being neither legitimate nor worthy."

Garrett was limited to the defense of serious criminal cases, mainly murder. "I am not entirely sure what first drew me to it but the fast-moving pace makes it more exciting than other areas of the law. I'd hold a gun to my own head before I'd practice real estate or corporate law. It simply would not hold my interest."

The highest-profile case he ever worked was known as "the Santa Claus murder." A young man was accused of slaughtering four members of a family as they slept and then abducting three little girls in a small hamlet called Santa Claus a hundred miles south of Augusta. The alleged perpetrator was an emotionally troubled young man in his early twenties. He had been a foster child to that same couple in that same house before leaving home some years earlier. But he had been secretly continuing a relationship with their sixteen-year-old daughter, who became one of his victims.

Garrett says: "Many people think that lawyers like me just walk onto a case, claim the state's purse and don't give a damn who wins or loses. Well, I know what it's like to have problem kids so at least I like to think I do care and I can relate to clients like Larry Kelley."

Garrett had bailed his own stepson out of more jails in Alabama and south Georgia than he cared to recall. The boy was still on the run when Garrett took on Larry Kelley's defense. As the attorney described his stepson: "He's held up gas stations, used loads of drugs. He's trouble. I know what it's like out there."

And Garrett was convinced that he understood the precise role his client had played in the murder of Kevin Spann.

Garrett had initially thought that Gina Spann had been in one of those marriages that simply petered out. Her husband held down three jobs and saved every penny he earned while his wife went off on her own crazy course through life.

Then Garrett concluded that Larry Kelley lacked a certain level of intelligence—which meant that he could be easily manipulated.

Garrett also felt it was significant that while Larry Kelley was living in Gina Spann's house in an adulterous relationship with an older married woman, he had with him the one thing that he really cared enough about to bring with him when he left home— his collection of dinosaurs. Little plastic and rubber toy animals. He was still a child.

Garrett knew that nobody in the case was squeaky

clean. But he firmly believed the evidence fell short of establishing that Larry Kelley actually participated in murder. "To me, Larry was effectively dropped from the conspiracy when he twice failed to kill Staff Sergeant Spann. From that point on, Larry was merely present but not a direct participant. He played a minimal role, even in the actual conspiracy, or plot," explained Garrett.

Garrett compared Larry Kelley's role to that of a lady in one of the many cases where the offender was a man and his girlfriend was just there, following him around. "She is in the car when he drives places and waits while he does things. Rarely are these girls prosecuted," said Garrett.

Garrett also believed that his client was so naive, he never appreciated the seriousness of what Gina Spann was planning. "Larry did not think very deeply. He'd never even had a girlfriend before. The guy was a virgin and she seduced him.

"This was sheer manipulation by a mature, seductive woman who provided him with experiences he probably had never even dreamt about. He was in love with her because she held him in awe of her."

But even Mike Garrett admitted that there were gross inconsistencies in Larry Kelley's relationship with Gina Spann.

"Mrs. Spann definitely felt a sort of protectiveness for Larry. I guess you'd call it a kind of loyalty. She didn't want to see him hurt too badly, she said.

"But once she told the police everything, there was little anyone could do to help her. The true strategy in going to trial was that at some point they would get a reduced charge."

Mike Garrett added: "Larry's problem was that he was not articulate or eloquent. To me it was very apparent that he couldn't really explain what had happened."

Garrett also did not hide his opinions about Larry Kelley's brother. "Michael Kelley did play a role in all this. He worked at the Taco Bell as well and Mrs. Spann did approach him about killing her husband before she eventually went to his brother.

"I even believe that Larry and his brother Michael together burglarized their stepfather's gun collection and one of those was used in the homicide. This case is riddled with holes."

Just a few weeks after Kevin Spann's murder, Larry Kelley's stepfather David Best died of a heart attack. Mike Garrett said about Larry's mother, "Not only did she have a son charged with murder but her husband died and both those kids were not doing so well at school. They ended up being school drop-outs working at Taco Bell. That says it all."

Garrett noticed how Kelley's mother tended to take a step back from the emotion of the situation and tried to hang onto what little she had in life. "You can't blame her, can you?" he surmised.

In the eyes of prosecutors led by DA Danny Craig, Mike Garrett's attitude was honorable if slightly misguided. But Garrett insisted: "I honestly try not to be judgmental because it doesn't help when you do what I do but the fact remains that Mrs. Spann was greedy and manipulative. She was willing to take unacceptable risks to obtain what she wanted. That makes her fairly unique whatever her true feelings for Larry might really be."

Mike Garrett saw Larry Kelley as being like a twig in a flooded stream, one of those streams they had a lot of in Georgia that are often swollen by rainstorms. He explained: "You throw one of those twigs or a branch in and quickly it's gone, it's nothing. You can't catch up to it and that's the end of it.

"It's so disturbing to me that Larry was just swept away by other people's manipulations and had his life destroyed because of it."

TWENTY-EIGHT

On Tuesday, June 3, 1997, a Richmond County grand jury indicted Gina Spann and the four teenagers accused of murdering Kevin Spann.

The indictment named Gina, Gerry Horne, Larry Kelley, Matt Piazzi and Chris Bargeron. Each was once again reminded that they had been charged with a felony murder, malice murder and use of a firearm during the commission of a crime.

No date for their trials were set.

Within a few days, prosecutors filed notice of their intentions to continue to seek the death penalty if a jury convicted Gina Spann of murder.

Gina and the elder two of her teenage co-defendants were to be arraigned the following Friday at Richmond County Superior Court.

It was clear that DA Danny Craig still wanted Gina Spann to pay the ultimate price for killing her husband.

Through the summer, Craig continued to pursue the death penalty until Gina Spann agreed to plead guilty to malice murder in exchange for the DA dropping the capital punishment option. Her decision would ultimately help speed up the trials.

By the fall of 1997 it was widely expected that the trials of Gina Spann and her four teenage co-defendants would be held before Christmas if the crowded Richmond County Superior Court could fit them in.

On November 21, 1997, Gina Spann pleaded guilty to malice murder and use of a firearm during the commission of a crime. At the last moment she had agreed to take a life-without-parole prison sentence to spare herself and Larry Kelley possible death sentences. She was sentenced to life in prison without parole, plus five years. The trial only lasted a couple of hours.

Gina Spann looked straight ahead without a flicker of emotion as the judge passed sentence. The trial was so brief it only made a few paragraphs in the local newspaper.

Of all the defendants, it was 16-year-old Chris Bargeron who emerged as the smartest.

From the moment he decided to accept Gina's "commission" to have Kevin Spann killed, Bargeron carefully distanced himself from the crime itself.

Initially, both Gina Spann and Larry Kelley had presumed that Bargeron would carry out the hit himself but he never had any intention of doing that.

He carefully asked around amongst his acquaintances until he found Gerry Horne. He then sized him up before deciding that he was the man for the job.

Although there is some confusion over exactly how much money Horne and then Piazzi would eventually get for the hit, there was no doubt that if they had all gotten away with it, Bargeron would have pocketed the majority of the cash.

Bargeron immediately fired a warning shot across the police bows by refusing to give a full statement of his involvement as all the others had.

So when Bargeron fell out with his state-appointed attorney it wasn't such a surprise that the teenager—then 17—opted to defend himself at his trial. As Larry Kelley's attorney Mike Garrett pointed out: "None of these kids were very clever but one of them—Bargeron—had a lot of animal cunning and he used it to good effect."

Bargeron himself looked anything but a cunning criminal. However, beneath his bloated exterior was a devious mind that served him well as he made Augusta legal history by becoming the youngest person ever to defend himself at a trial connected with a murder.

Bargeron explained it like this: "I wasn't worried about defending myself even when the judge warned me I faced a mandatory sentence for life imprisonment if convicted." And he meant it.

In fact the judge even warned Bargeron when he announced he was dispensing with the services of his state-provided defender: "They know their business . . . you want to give all that up? Are you prepared to go to prison? Is that what you are telling the court?"

Bargeron nodded his head at the judge. Many older people would have thought twice about it. But as one old Butler High School friend pointed out: "Chris Bargeron always had his own agenda. He didn't try hard in class but you always knew that he had the answers. He just saw himself as being above it all."

Bargeron was so clued up he even filed a motion just before his own trial seeking the removal of Chief

Judge William M. Fleming Jr. and Judge Bernard Mulherin Sr., who were scheduled to preside over his hearing.

Bargeron's reasoning for this sounded like the words of a fully trained attorney: "I felt the cases were not properly assigned in the Augusta Judicial Circuit and the judges had improper, one-sided communications with the district attorney concerning the assignment of the cases."

Bargeron's move stunned the court but there wasn't a lot they could do about it. Bargeron had cleverly spent much of his five months in prison reading law books at the rate of one every two days.

Bargeron himself got the idea about seeking the removal of the judges from a previous case he'd read about.

He explained: "It involved a guy called William Lumpkin who faced capital murder charges over the September 2, 1996, death of a real estate agent. Mr. Lumpkin's lawyers argued that local judges did not follow Georgia Supreme Court rules that required the clerk's office to assign cases to judges on equal basis."

Bargeron's legal move was eventually thrown out. But he claimed one of the main reasons was because he had to hand-write all his legal motions and letters which were then filed in the court clerk's office.

"But I sure made a point that everyone took notice of," he later said.

Bargeron's basic aim was to insure that he got a separate trial from the rest of the defendants because he knew that he could then possibly get off on lesser charges. He succeeded.

The teenager cannily offered to help the police

without implicating himself. Bargeron got them to agree not to prosecute him for murder like all the other defendants.

Chris Bargeron pleaded guilty to conspiracy and was sentenced to five years in prison followed by five years probation. Considering that all his co-defendants faced a minimum of life in prison, Bargeron's sentence was a good result.

Bargeron's own comments on his experiences as an amateur attorney summed up his mentality: "I learned a lot of stuff out there in that courtroom. I understood the risks from both the prosecutors and the other defending attorneys. I knew they might try to put all the blame on me for Sergeant Spann's slaying."

One attorney who was present during Bargeron's trial couldn't help being impressed. "Bargeron is a waste of talent. That kid is one of the brightest young defendants we've ever had in this court."

Bargeron himself was extremely proud of his status and with a certain amount of arrogance he said: "They reckon I was probably the youngest person in Georgia to represent myself on a murder charge. They knew I had the right and there wasn't a damn thing they could do about it."

He went on: "Far as I'm concerned if a person is old enough to face a criminal charge as an adult then I was old enough to make my own decision about legal representation. In Georgia any person 17 and over faces criminal charges as an adult."

According to Mike Garrett one of the biggest inconsistencies in the case was that Bargeron—the man who subcontracted the killing out—was allowed to plead to facilitation to murder, which only carried a five-year sentence. "Yet Larry Kelley never agreed to kill anyone and did not pull the trigger. He was simply there," said an angry Garrett after Bargeron's sentencing. "This was not a straightforward crime. They didn't just walk into a gas station and shoot someone."

Bargeron's bargaining edge was that he was the only one who did not confess all to the police on the night of the murder when he was arrested. The others talked and talked even though they were advised of their rights to remain silent. That's where Bargeron's cunning played a crucial role.

As Mike Garrett explained: "Everyone was looked in the eye by their police interrogators and told: 'You talk to me if you want to but every word you say is going to be used against you.' It seems that only one actually took any notice of them.

"All the other defendants talked. But that one boy who remained silent knew that because of his knowledge of the actual shooters and Mrs. Spann's role in the killing he had a bargaining chip to use and it would have been difficult to prove the case against him because of a lack of a confession."

Garrett still insisted that Larry Kelley was innocent: "As far as I am concerned Larry Kelley was dropped from the murder conspiracy because he twice failed to carry through on Mrs. Spann's plots for her husband's demise.

"That evidence was just not there. I think he was far less involved than Mr. Bargeron, who's only serving five years."

*   *   *

Chris Bargeron knew he'd achieved quite an impressive result thanks to his own do-it-yourself style of defending.

As one attorney commented: "Five years as opposed to life in prison is a result any lawyer would be proud of."

Bargeron himself even admitted after the sentencing: "In the end I reckon I did okay. I pleaded guilty to conspiracy and got five years followed by five years probation."

On November 29, 1997, it was being predicted in the reliable *Augusta Chronicle* that the three remaining teenagers could go on trial as early as the following Monday.

On Monday, December 1, 1997, Matt Piazzi pleaded guilty to gunning down Kevin Spann. Piazzi—who'd turned 17 while awaiting trial—was sentenced to the mandatory life sentence for felony murder.

In exchange for his guilty plea and willingness to testify against Kelley and Horne, malice murder and weapon violation charges against Piazzi were dropped by the DA.

On Friday, December 5, Gerry Horne pleaded guilty to felony murder and was sentenced to life in prison. Charges of malice murder and possession of a firearm during the commission of certain crimes were also dropped in exchange for his plea after yet another deal with DA Danny Craig.

Larry Kelley's trial finally kicked off on Monday, December 8. He had elected to go for jury trial after pleading not guilty to felony murder, malice murder and use of a firearm during the commission of a crime.

The following day Kelley took the witness stand in his own defense, telling the jury that Kevin Spann's murder was Gina Spann's idea.

Mike Garrett tried to convince the jury that Kelley had been dropped from the murder conspiracy because he'd twice failed to go through with Gina Spann's plots for her husband's demise.

Chris Bargeron even testified at Larry Kelley's trial that Gina Spann offered him money to help kill her husband. "Me and Larry tried twice but couldn't go through with it. That's when I suggested I might know someone who would do it," Bargeron told the jury.

But DA Danny Craig was adamant that Larry Kelley had to take full responsibility for his actions.

"I think it was obvious he was a primary perpetrator of the crime. Larry Kelley was not just the duped boyfriend along for the ride as has been suggested. As long as there's a breath of life in me, I will fight to keep this man [Kelley] in the penitentiary—forever. I think that's the least a citizen can do for a person who has given his life in service to this country."

It was all good, stirring, patriotic stuff from Danny Craig, who went on to tell the jurors: "The issue in this case is whether this defendant [Kelley] joined in the conspiracy . . . and if Kevin Spann was murdered as a result of that agreement."

As a party to a crime, surmised Craig, "Mr. Kelley was just as guilty of murder as Mr. Piazzi or Mr. Horne or Ms. Spann, because he was there from the beginning of the conspiracy to kill Staff Sergeant Spann, and he stayed in the conspiracy through the fourth attempt, which proved fatally successful."

There was a flat atmosphere inside the court on the actual day of Larry's sentencing. To many it was a foregone conclusion. Mitigating circumstances were deemed irrelevant because there was only one sentence the judge could impose—life plus five years for possession of a firearm during the commission of the crime. In other words, they said that at some moment he had possession of the gun. The earliest Kelley could make parole was in the year 2011.

Attorney Mike Garrett was disappointed. "I stopped blaming myself for Larry Kelley's incarceration a long time ago. I try so many murder cases that there is little room for remorse. But there has to be more give and take within contemporary America for prosecutorial discretion to be exercised. Judges and prosecutors sometimes seem more interested in headlines than true justice.

"Most folk think it's a very black-and-white situation. They really don't want to know about the Gina Spanns and the Larry Kelleys of this world. They just want them put away to rot in a prison where crime rules more than it does in the outside world but at least the normal people don't have to deal with it."

DA Danny Craig had a different take on the Kelley trial: "I think it was obvious to the jury that this wasn't a duped boyfriend, but a primary perpetrator of the crime. I think this jury was highly offended by the notion that a young gangster sat in judgment of a veteran of Desert Storm . . . I know I was."

*   *   *

Three months after taking a life-without-parole prison sentence to spare herself and Larry Kelley possible death sentences, Gina Spann returned to court claiming that her sentence had been too harsh.

Defense attorneys Maureen Floyd and her colleague Richard Ingram contended that life without parole was unconstitutional and should be dropped.

They later recalled: "We went back to the court because we believed Gina's sentence was too harsh. Okay, so our earlier plea agreement spared her the death sentence, but we contended that life without parole was unconstitutional under the circumstances and it should have been abolished. If that happened we would have challenged the original sentence."

Richard Ingram had an interesting take on the personality of so-called brutal killer Gina Spann: "I found Gina very highly strung and definitely not the cold fish that many have tried to make out she is. She did a lot of crying during our interviews.

"Gina seemed to be fighting a lot of inner turmoil. Maybe that was because she knew so many things about this case which she felt she could not tell us about."

DA Danny Craig naturally disagreed. He told the court: "It would be unfair to the public to allow the motion to sit, possibly for years, while the prosecution's case weakened with age. That's why I asked the judge to either dismiss the motion or nullify Mrs. Spann's plea and sentence and allow the state to try Mrs. Spann."

DA Danny Craig pointed out that Gina Spann's plea negotiation had specifically stated that she was giving up her right to any appeal and if she did challenge her sentence then she could yet stand trial on capital murder charges.

Judge Bernard J. Mulherin Sr. dismissed the motion on Monday, February 16, 1998, and Gina went back to jail for what looked like the rest of her life.

Meanwhile Kevin Spann's ex-girlfriend approached insurers to make a claim on his policies because she had had a child by him before he married Gina. At the time of writing, the insurance companies were considering her claim and that of Gina's sister who was trying to get a share of the money for Kevin Spann's stepson Michael.

At the end of 1998, Larry Kelley's attorney Mike Garrett announced he was still planning an appeal for his client although he knew it would be an uphill task. "To be entirely honest about it, I *never* feel confident about an appeal. I'm better at predicting juries than I am at predicting what our supreme court might decide.

"I suppose Larry expected what happened at the trial. That emotional deadness we talked about earlier prevented him from even considering any other verdict and sentence.

"There is an appeal due to go in and once I get the full transcript of the trial I can take this thing forward. The first stage in that appeal will be a motion for a new trial. At that point a lot of issues in the appeal will be clarified and then we might start to actually make some sense of this whole sorry business."

AFTERWORD

Society generally holds that murder for hire is one of the most heinous forms of killing. Involvement in a so-called "hit" is one of the few "special circumstances" categories of homicide which can provoke prosecution pleas for the death penalties in many states across the nation. This applies to those who get paid as well as those who hire the killers.

No one knows exactly how many people are killed by hired assassins each year, but it must be safe to say that it is still only a small percentage of the total number of murders committed. Nevertheless, it is a growing problem.

Admittedly, little is known about the minds and driving forces behind hired killers in general. News reports focus more on the murders that have been committed than on who's behind the crime.

In the imaginary world of novels and movies, hit-men are often portrayed as cold and calculating. Even the euphemisms used to describe what they do have a mechanical ring to them: *hit*, *terminate*, *rub-out*, *eliminate*. They are expected to be efficient, highly knowledgeable about their intended victims' schedules and those people's private and public habits. We presume the would-be killers move in a shadowy world, living anonymously amongst law-abiding citizens who are completely unaware of their neighbor's "career." They are careful always to avoid working inside their home territory because that would be deemed amateurish and extremely risky.

But in the real world, as you will have found out reading this book, killing for hire is anything but a carefully executed crime carried out by shrewd, ruthless individuals. Instead, the young killers of Kevin Spann seemed to be driven by an abject desperation for a relatively modest sum of money which caused their crime to be punctuated by sloppiness and chaos. If it wasn't so tragic it would have been sheer comedy.

But what makes the killing of Gulf War vet Staff Sergeant Kevin Spann so fascinating is the complex interplay of the characters for whom life centered around a fast-food joint and an older woman whose tragic past manifested itself in a brutal and bloody murder.

The characters in this sad saga are so normal it begins to make you wonder if they are really not much different from your own family and friends.

Boredom, educational failure, easy access to firearms and the sort of emotional void that seems to fill so many younger people these days combined to deadly effect.

STILL ZONED OUT— AN EPILOGUE

CHRIS BARGERON remains very aloof from the three other youths who are bitter about the light sentence he received. Bargeron has told prison visitors that he is seriously hoping to work in the field of law when he is released in the year 2002.

DANNY CRAIG's reputation as the Augusta District Attorney continues to rise and he is adamant that Gina Spann will never get an early release from prison.

JESSE DUNN now has a secure full-time job at a computer store and says he never wants to see or hear from Gina Spann ever again.

MAUREEN FLOYD continues to represent Gina Spann and is currently moving forward with her plans to appeal against her client's sentencing despite the judge's ruling in February 1998.

MIKE GARRETT continues to prepare an appeal for his client Larry Kelley but he is far from optimistic that it will succeed.

MICHAEL HILL is now 14 years old and lives with his Aunt Jody Pierce—Gina's sister—at her home in Belleville, Illinois.

LARRY KELLEY, MATT PIAZZI AND GERRY HORNE are said by authorities to be extremely quiet, model prisoners. And those who have visited them at the Richmond County Youth Detention Center say the three youths are completely "zoned out" about the crime they committed. They still don't seem to fully realize what they did.

JODY PIERCE is currently trying to claim some of Kevin Spann's life-insurance money to be used for his stepson Michael. She says she never wants to see her sister again.

SUE PIERCE is still too shocked to talk about the crime her daughter committed and lives quietly in Belleville, Illinois.

AMANDA QUICK continues to dine out on her "fifteen minutes of fame" following her appearance on a *Hard Copy* special on the Spann case. Since the murder she has become one of Augusta's numerous teenage moms.

GINA SPANN still is the only one who knows precisely why she wanted to murder her husband. Despite intensive psychotherapy in prison she has never shared a full account of the death of her husband. She also continues to insist she is innocent.

JIMMY VOWELL has never since managed to solve a murder at the speed with which he cracked the Kevin Spann slaying. He has moved off the serious crimes unit at C.I.D. but is edging closer to celebrating twenty years on the force.

THE SENTENCES

GINA SPANN is serving a life sentence without parole plus five years.

LARRY KELLEY, the boyfriend who twice tried but failed to carry out Gina Spann's murder plots, is now serving a life sentence.

MATT PIAZZI, the triggerman who agreed the night before the slaying to commit murder, is serving a life sentence.

GERALD HORNE, who agreed to kill Staff Sgt. Spann and was present when the murder happened, is serving a life sentence.

CHRISTOPHER BARGERON pleaded guilty to conspiracy and received a five-year prison sentence followed by a five-year probationary sentence.

ABOUT THE AUTHOR

WENSLEY CLARKSON has written thirty-one books—which have sold more than a million copies worldwide—including the tabloid newspaper exposé *Dog Eat Dog*, biographies of John Travolta and Quentin Tarantino, plus fifteen best-selling true-crime books including *Doctors of Death*, *Whatever Mother Says*, *Deadly Seduction*, *Slave Girls*, *Death at Every Stop*, *In the Name of Satan*, *The Railroad Killer* and *Caged Heat*.

Too dangerous for society
Too close for comfort
Too hot to handle

CAGED HEAT

The True Story of Female Murderers Behind Bars

Wensley Clarkson

They were once sweet little girls—sugar and spice, and everything nice. Now they're cold-blooded killers, behind the bars of America's most dangerous prisons—hardened criminals doing their time. How and why did these women cross to the dark side; what made them murder husbands, lovers, family, innocent strangers; and what is life like when you're locked up with volatile killers in your own personal hell? From their illicit love affairs to race relations, prostitution, protection rackets and drug smuggling—all in prison—author Wensley Clarkson has used his unique, unlimited access to some of America's toughest prisons to reveal the shocking story of women who kill...and the world they now call home.

CH 3/00

NEXT STOP, MURDER...

THE
RAILROAD
KILLER

The Shocking True Story of Eight Gruesome
Murders and the Man Suspected of
Committing Them

WENSLEY CLARKSON

Angel Maturino Resendez is described by most who know him as
a quiet, polite, soft-spoken man, a loving husband and father to a
baby daughter. But law enforcement officials suspect that he
might be responsible for upwards of eight grisly and random
killings in a span of two years, all of which occurred near the
southwest railroad line that the killer is believed to have ridden on
his twisted murder spree. In each case, the same mode of attack—
and the same slow and painful death—appears to have been used,
pointing to the methodical slayings of a serial killer. Is Angel
Maturino Resendez the ruthless Railroad Killer—a sadistic slayer
who led police on one of the longest manhunts in history?
Bestselling true crime author Wensley Clarkson digs deep into the
heart of a horrifying murder case to uncover some stunning
answers.

They'd do anything to win their mother's love.
But would they kill their own sisters?

WHATEVER MOTHER SAYS...

A True Story of a Mother, Madness and Murder

Wensley Clarkson

Raising her five kids alone in a rundown section of
Sacramento, Theresa Cross Knorr seemed like the ultimate
survivor. But her youngest daughter, 16-year-old Terry, told
police another story. According to Terry, Theresa—no
longer the petite brunette she once was—had turned insane-
ly jealous of her pretty eldest daughters and enlisted the
help of her two teenaged sons in a vicious campaign against
their sisters. Terry's gruesome tale tells how Theresa had
drugged, handcuffed and shot 16-year-old Suesan, allowing
her wounds to fester, until she ordered her sons to burn their
sister alive. Next, according to Terry, her mother savagely
beat 20-year-old Sheila and locked her in a broom closet,
where she would starve to death. Here, in vivid detail, is the
shocking account of Theresa Cross Knorr, a woman who
might just be the mother of all murderesses...